THE MUSICIAN'S GUIDE TO AURAL SKILLS

Volume 1

Sight-Singing, Rhythm-Reading, Improvisation, and Keyboard Skills

Joel Phillips
Westminster Choir College of Rider University

Paul Murphy
State University of New York at Fredonia

Elizabeth West Marvin
Eastman School of Music

Jane Piper Clendinning
Florida State University College of Music

W. W. NORTON & COMPANY
NEW YORK · LONDON

W. W. Norton & Company has been independent since its founding in 1923, when William Warder Norton and Mary D. Herter Norton first began to publish lectures delivered at the People's Institute, the adult education division of New York City's Cooper Union. The firm soon expanded its program beyond the Institute, publishing books by celebrated academics from America and abroad. By midcentury, the two major pillars of Norton's publishing program—trade books and college texts—were firmly established. In the 1950s, the Norton family transferred control of the company to its employees, and today—with a staff of four hundred and a comparable number of trade, college, and professional titles published each year—W. W. Norton & Company stands as the largest and oldest publishing house owned wholly by its employees.

Copyright © 2011/2005 by W. W. Norton & Company, Inc.

All rights reserved
Printed in the United States of America
First Edition

Editor: Maribeth Payne
Developmental editor: Susan Gaustad
Managing editor, College: Marian Johnson
E-media editor: Steve Hoge
Assistant editor: Ariella Foss
Production manager: Benjamin Reynolds
Manufacturing by Quad/Graphics—Dubuque, IA
Music typesetting and page composition: Willow Graphics / David Botwinik; TexTech
Art director: Hope Miller Goodell
Book design: Lisa Buckley and Rubina Yeh

Library of Congress Cataloging-in-Publication Data

Phillips, Joel, 1958–
   The musician's guide to aural skills / Joel Phillips, Paul Murphy, Elizabeth West Marvin,
Jane Piper Clendinning. — 2nd ed.
      v. cm.
   Includes index.

   ISBN 978-0-393-93094-8 (pbk., v. 1) — **ISBN 978-0-393-93095-5** (pbk., v. 2)

  1. Ear training. 2. Music theory—Elementary works. I. Murphy, Paul, 1962–
II. Clendinning, Jane Piper. III. Marvin, Elizabeth West, 1955– IV. Title.
  MT35.P49 2012
  781.4'24—dc23

W. W. Norton & Company, Inc., 500 Fifth Avenue, New York, N. Y. 10110
www.wwnorton.com
W. W. Norton & Company Ltd., Castle House, 75/76 Wells Street, London W1T 3QT

2 3 4 5 6 7 8 9 0

Contents

Part III   Chromatic Harmony and Form

Part IV   The Twentieth Century and Beyond

Improvisation 381

Keyboard Skills   405

Preface

The *Musician's Guide* series is the most comprehensive set of materials available for learning music theory. This book, *The Musician's Guide to Aural Skills* (in two volumes) teaches the practical skills you need as a professional musician—dictation, sight-singing, rhythm-reading, keyboard harmony, improvisation, and composition—and allows you to hear every concept in the context of music literature. Though the book corresponds to its companion text, *The Musician's Guide to Theory and Analysis*, Second Edition, it can be used by itself or in conjunction with other theory texts. The Second Edition of *Aural Skills* is organized in two volumes:

> ***Volume 1, Sight-Singing, Rhythm-Reading, Improvisation, and Keyboard Skills***, emphasizes the skills required for real-time performances. The content of each section corresponds to blocks of chapters in *The Musician's Guide to Theory and Analysis* (Second Edition), and provides enough flexibility to enable you to learn essential skills at your own pace.

> ***Volume 2, Ear-Training and Composition***, develops listening and writing skills in assignments that you may complete outside of class. Corresponding chapter-by-chapter to *The Musician's Guide to Theory and Analysis*, the ear-training is divided into two activities: "Inductive Listening" (short, preparatory model dictations that you can self-check) and "Contextual Listening" (dictations from music literature carefully selected to emphasize a chapter's concepts). All dictations are included on the accompanying Recordings DVD. A final section, "Composition," guides you from the very beginning through individual and group compositions in a variety of styles.

The Musician's Guide to Aural Skills is distinctive in three significant ways. First, it integrates skills you need in order to understand common musical patterns. These include the ability to imagine and perform the sounds of printed music; to recall music you hear by singing, playing, and writing it; and to demonstrate your grasp of a variety of musical styles in order to create and perform similar music of your own. Second, all contextual-listening and most sight-singing examples are from music literature, not contrived. Using real music examples encourages you to learn by listening to and imitating the music of diverse composers who wrote in a variety of styles, from classical to popular. Third, music for sight-singing and rhythm-reading includes many ensemble works—not only duets, but also music for three, four, and five parts.

Using These Volumes

Volume 1: Sight-Singing, Rhythm-Reading, Improvisation, and Keyboard Skills

As you move through each section in volume 1, we indicate how the materials correspond to the chapters in all other parts of *The Musician's Guide* series.

The initial sight-singing melodies are études specifically composed to help you acclimate to singing and conducting, to recognize and interpret the visual elements of music notation, and to develop a sense of scale degree and intonation by applying solfège syllables or scale-degree numbers. You will want to return to these études throughout your study, using them for warm-ups, syllable mastery, and vocal development. Most of the remaining melodies are drawn from a wide range of music literature—from popular (Broadway musicals, movies and television, classic rock, jazz, and blues) as well as common-practice music literature.

While *The Musician's Guide to Theory and Analysis* provides an overview of rhythmic concepts and terminology, this book emphasizes the practical application of reading and performing rhythms. The hundreds of exercises here are graduated so that you can learn to recognize patterns in a sequential fashion. We have provided corresponding chapter indications to *Theory and Analysis* to guide you through the rhythms.

We also offer a series of lessons in improvisation, an important and creative aspect of making music. The lessons feature enough scaffolding so that even if you have never improvised before, you can succeed in this key skill and have fun in the process. These exercises, for both solo and group performance, are designed to reinforce key concepts in music theory.

Finally, we reinforce all musical concepts at the keyboard. Our purpose here is not to develop pianists, but rather to teach you how to realize the sounds and ideas you study with this most fundamental musical tool. While everyone should be able to play the easiest exercises, you should *try* to play all of them: it is important to learn to play as much as you can as soon as you can. Designed to help you master harmonic and voice-leading patterns, these lessons are precisely matched to volume 2's inductive-listening and composition exercises as well as to this volume's improvisations. The keyboard exercises progress in a spiral fashion, often returning to earlier models to demonstrate and facilitate more advanced aspects of keyboard harmony. For example, simple two-voice contrapuntal patterns return later as the soprano and bass of four-part exercises, and even later with chromatic alterations. Spiral learning demonstrates the simple origins of what might otherwise seem complex.

Volume 2: Ear-Training and Composition

In volume 2, the ear-training activities are organized into forty chapters that correspond to the same-numbered chapters in all other *Musician's Guide* materials. All recorded examples are found on the DVD that accompanies this volume. For best results, plug headphones, earbuds, or external speakers into your computer's audio output jack; a laptop's built-in speakers will not adequately reproduce the lower pitches.

Each chapter begins with "Inductive Listening." These self-led, self-evaluated short dictations reinforce chapter concepts as well as rhythm, melody, counterpoint, and harmony. This section, which includes blank staves to help you get started, also prepares you to take the longer dictations from music literature called "Contextual Listening."

The "Contextual Listening" is a uniquely powerful feature of this book. Carefully selected from instrumental, vocal, chamber, and orchestral literature, these dictations, organized by level of difficulty, demonstrate concepts from each new chapter while reinforcing those from previous chapters. Each music example is accompanied by exercises that help guide your listening—from multiple-choice questions about form, meter, rhythm, cadence, or sequence types to questions that ask you to write what you hear with solfège syllables or with notation on a staff. There are enough exercises here to enable you to master this essential skill while providing challenges as well.

"Contextual Listening" assignments are designed to be completed outside of class, but your teacher may begin an example in class in order to check significant elements such as key and meter, and then assign the remaining exercises for homework. We encourage you to listen to each example as many times as you wish. For some of the more challenging works, consider working with a partner or play what you hear on an instrument. These contextual-listening exercises could be the most challenging, yet most valuable, aspect of your study. The main goal is to develop and improve your strategies for thinking and listening. Don't be discouraged if you don't get everything right. It takes time to develop these skills.

The final "Composition" section teaches you to apply the theoretical concepts you have learned through individual and group composition in a variety of styles. Performing and listening to your own creative work and that of your peers can be an exciting and rewarding experience.

The Recordings DVD that accompanies this volume is organized by chapter; each chapter includes two folders, one for "Inductive Listening" (IL) and the other for "Contextual Listening" (CL). The IL folder contains audio files paired with the corresponding notation for each exercise so that you can check your understanding immediately. An index for each chapter provides instructions and orientation to each dictation, allowing you to work on your own.

Applying Solfège Syllables and Scale-Degree Numbers

We maintain that all singing systems have merit and that choosing *some* system is far superior to using none. To reinforce musical patterns, we recommend singing with movable-*do* solfège syllables and/or scale-degree numbers. In the most common form of movable *do*, the tonic pitch in major or minor keys is always called *do*. Movable *do* helps demonstrate tonal patterns common to all keys; because there are no consonant blends and the vowels are pure, solfège can help produce a better vocal tone. Singing with scale-degree numbers is analogous to using movable *do*.

Some musicians sing *do* on *any* form of C regardless of the key; this system is called fixed *do*. Fixed *do* is an excellent tool for approximating absolute pitch. Singing with letter names is analogous to singing with fixed *do*. To use the fixed-*do* system with this book, we recommend that you ignore the movable-*do* solfège syllables, reinforce tonal patterns by singing with scale-degree numbers, and sing at sight with fixed-*do* syllables.

Diatonic syllables and numbers in major keys (Chapter 1)
All vowels are pronounced as in Italian. Sing "sev" on scale-degree seven to maintain proper rhythm.

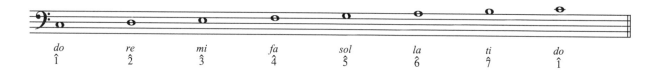

Chromatic syllables and numbers, major keys (begin as early as Chapter 2, but not later than Chapter 5)

In major keys other than C, the scale-degree symbols ♯ and ♭ mean "raised" and "lowered," respectively. For example, in B♭ major (below), the second and seventh notes are written with ♮, but their scale-degree numbers are ♯1̂ and ♯4̂.

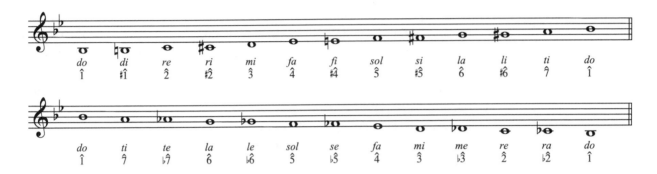

Chromatic syllables and numbers, minor keys and modes (Chapter 5)

In minor keys and modes, solfège syllables are assigned as if the music were written in the major key with the same tonic or final, as shown in this D minor example.

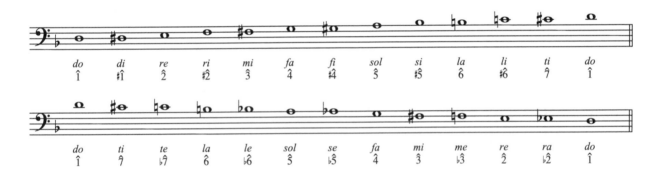

Applying a Rhythm-Counting System

Many people use some counting system when performing rhythms—in effect, "rhythmic solfège." For example, the rhythm ♩ might be vocalized du de, du ta de ta; or 1 and, 2 e and a, in $\frac{2}{4}$ meter. The most rational and sophisticated counting system is called Takadimi. Developed by Richard Hoffman, William Pelto, and John W. White, Takadimi is described at their website (http://takadimi.net), which includes a downloadable short guide. We leave it to the discretion of each instructor whether to require such a system and which to require.

The *Musician's Guide* Series

The Second Edition of the *Musician's Guide* series provides the theoretical foundation and the practical musicianship skills you need to become a well-rounded, versatile musician. *Theory and Analysis* covers all the topics necessary for a comprehensive two-year program in music theory, from fundamentals to post-tonal analysis. *Aural Skills* integrates and applies the critical aural skills in a program carefully coordinated to reinforce all essential theoretical concepts. Together, this series completes a comprehensive theory and aural skills curriculum.

For Instructors

For faculty who adopt *The Musician's Guide to Aural Skills*, the Teacher's Edition of volume 2 provides answers for all exercises, thus serving as a valuable dictation manual, plus indispensable strategies that help convey important concepts. An invaluable resource to all instructors, the Teacher's Edition is especially useful to those for whom music theory is a secondary area or who are new to the profession. There are enough assignments so that you might reserve some for quizzes or for make-up work, or ask more experienced students to complete the most difficult exercises and those with less experience to complete the easier ones.

The main goal of the "Contextual Listening" assignments is to develop and improve students' strategies for thinking and listening. Striving for perfection is admirable, but students shouldn't be discouraged if they don't get everything right. For that reason, you might evaluate this work in a more holistic manner, focusing on whether students have understood the main concepts of an exercise, rather than on every small detail of their answers. For some of the more challenging exercises, allow students to work with a partner. Long examples, such as those for invention, fugue, and sonata, may be assigned in parts; check the work on each part before assigning the next one.

The Teacher's Edition of volume 2 includes scores for all "Contextual Listening" examples, together with answer keys and strategies for presentation of the material. You may also wish to use the "Inductive Listening" notation included on the Recordings DVD for additional in-class drill and practice.

Planning Your Curriculum

The Musician's Guide covers concepts typically taught during the first two years of college instruction in music. In addition to serving the needs of the college curriculum, the *Musician's Guide* series is also ideal for anyone who teaches similar courses in secondary schools. In particular, Parts I and II, covering "Elements of Music" and "Diatonic Harmony and Tonicization," correspond to the content of the Advanced Placement Course in Music Theory®, featuring comparable terminology, exercises, and listening activities.

For instructors who adopt both the *Theory and Analysis* and *Aural Skills* texts, we know you will appreciate the consistent pedagogical approach, terminology, and order of presentation that the two texts share. Nevertheless, you may find at times that students' aural and practical skills develop more slowly than their initial grasp of theoretical concepts. There is no harm done if aural/practical instruction trails slightly behind conceptual understanding. For this reason, we summarize the organization of the volumes and suggest several strategies for using them.

Typically deployed over four or five semesters, most college curricula might be addressed by one of the two models shown below.

Plan 1 (four semesters)

	Volume 1	Volume 2
Term 1	Part I, including Improvisation Lessons 1–7 and Keyboard Lessons 1–7.	Chapters 1–10 and Compositions 1–4.
Term 2	Part II, including Improvisation Lessons 8–15 and Keyboard Lessons 8–16.	Chapters 11–21 and Compositions 5–11.
Term 3	Part III, including Improvisation Lessons 16–20 and Keyboard Lessons 17–20.	Chapters 22–32 and Compositions 12–13.
Term 4	Part IV, including Improvisation Lessons 21–25 and Keyboard Lesson 21.	Chapters 33–40 and Compositions 14–17.

Alternatively, the following organization is one suggestion for those curricula that offer a dedicated rudiments class.

Plan 2 (a rudiments class followed by four semesters)

	Volume 1	Volume 2
Rudiments Class	Part I (omitting modal melodies and beat subdivisions): Sight-Singing sections A and B; Rhythm-Reading sections A and B; Improvisation Lessons 1–3 and 5; Keyboard Lessons 1–2, 4–5, and 6.	Chapters 1–8 and Compositions 1–2.
Term 1	Part I: Sight-Singing sections C and D; Rhythm-Reading sections C–E; Improvisation Lessons 4 and 6–7; Keyboard Lessons 3 and 7. Part II: Sight-Singing sections A and B; Rhythm-Reading sections A and B; Improvisation Lessons 8–12; Keyboard Lessons 8–13.	Chapters 9–17 (with review of modes from Chapter 3) and Compositions 3–7.
Term 2	Part II: Sight-Singing sections C and D; Rhythm-Reading sections C–G; Improvisation Lessons 13–15; Keyboard Lessons 14–17. Part III: Sight-Singing section A.	Chapters 18–24 and Compositions 8–11.
Term 3	Part III: Sight-Singing sections B and C; Rhythm-Reading for Part III (complete); Improvisation Lessons 16–20; Keyboard Lessons 18–20.	Chapters 25–32 and Compositions 12–13.
Term 4	Part IV: Sight-Singing and Rhythm-Reading for Part IV (complete); Improvisation Lessons 21–25; Keyboard Lesson 21.	Chapters 33–40 and Compositions 14–17.

Each volume in *Aural Skills* is sufficiently self-contained that it may be used individually, or in conjunction with theory texts besides *The Musician's Guide to Theory and Analysis*, 2/e. In addition, the *MacGAMUT* ear-training and dictation software program (www .macgamut.com) now includes a specially prepared curriculum pre-set to correspond with the *Musician's Guide* texts.

Our Thanks to . . .

A work of this size and scope is helped along the way by many people. We are especially grateful for the support of our families and our students. Our work together as co-authors has been incredibly rewarding, and we are thankful for that collaboration.

For subvention of the recordings, we thank James Undercofler (director and dean of the Eastman School of Music), as well as Eastman's Professional Development Committee. For CD engineering, we are grateful to recording engineers John Ebert and John Baker. For CD production work, we thank Glenn West, Christina Lenti, and Lance Peeler, who assisted in the recording sessions. We also thank our colleagues at both Westminster Choir College of Rider University and the Eastman School of Music who gave of their talents to help make the recordings. The joy of their music making contributed mightily to this project.

We are grateful for the thorough and detailed work of our prepublication reviewers, whose suggestions inspired many improvements, large and small: Melissa Cox, Emory University; Jeff Donovick, St. Petersburg College; Bruce Hammel, Virginia Commonwealth University; Tim Pack, University of Oregon; Ruth Rendleman, Montclair State University; Alexander Tutunov, Southern Oregon University; and Annie K. Yih, University of California at Santa Barbara.

We are indebted to the W.W. Norton staff for their commitment to this project and their painstaking care in producing these volumes. Most notable among these are developmental editor Susan Gaustad, whose knowledge of music and detailed, thoughtful questions made her a joy to work with, and music editor Maribeth Anderson Payne, whose vision has helped launch the new edition with great enthusiasm. We appreciate the invaluable assistance of media expert Steve Hoge and the careful listening skills of Kate Maroney. Thanks also to typesetters David Botwinik and Kathleen Richards, to Justin Hoffman, and to Ben Reynolds for overseeing the book's production.

Joel Phillips, Paul Murphy, Elizabeth West Marvin, and Jane Piper Clendinning

Elements of Music

Sight-Singing

A. Major Keys, Simple Meters (Chapters 1–3)

This section features simple-meter melodies with quarter- and half-note beat units, in keys ranging from three flats to three sharps. Sing with solfège syllables, scale-degree numbers, and/or letter names. Sing hollow note heads longer than filled ones.

C major scale plus *ti* ($\hat{7}$) and *re* ($\hat{2}$), treble and bass clefs

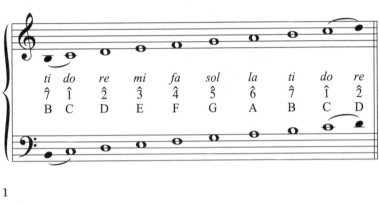

7

8

9

10

11

12

13

C major scale plus *sol–la–ti* ($\hat{5}$–$\hat{6}$–$\hat{7}$) and *re* ($\hat{2}$), alto and tenor clefs

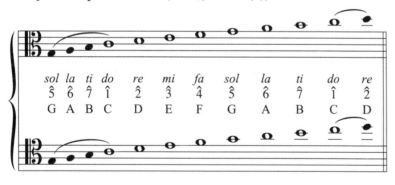

sol	la	ti	do	re	mi	fa	sol	la	ti	do	re
$\hat{5}$	$\hat{6}$	$\hat{7}$	$\hat{1}$	$\hat{2}$	$\hat{3}$	$\hat{4}$	$\hat{5}$	$\hat{6}$	$\hat{7}$	$\hat{1}$	$\hat{2}$
G	A	B	C	D	E	F	G	A	B	C	D

14

15

Of the following simple-duple-meter melodies, the first sixteen are grouped in pairs. Though their tonic pitches differ, each of the paired melodies should be sung with identical solfège syllables or scale-degree numbers.

Sing *do* ($\hat{1}$), the final pitch of each melody, then sing up or down to find *sol* ($\hat{5}$), the anacrusis.

In cut-time melodies, because the half note gets one beat, remember to conduct each measure in two.

C major pentatonic scale

Music from the Literature

111   Richard Rodgers, "Bye and Bye"

112 Donovan, "Brother Sun, Sister Moon"

113 "Oh, How Lovely Is the Evening" (traditional; round in three parts)

114 "My Country, 'Tis of Thee" (traditional)

Many melodies begin on a pitch other than the tonic, often on *sol* ($\hat{5}$) or *mi* ($\hat{3}$). Find the tonic, then sing to the starting pitch.

115 Gustav Mahler, Symphony No. 2, first movement (adapted)

116 "Hot Cross Buns" (traditional)

117 Béla Bartók, No. 1 from *44 Duets*, vol. I

118 A. Emmett Adams, "The Bells of St. Mary's"

119 Jerome Kern, "Look for the Silver Lining"

120 Dick Miles, "The Coffee Song"

121 Gene Autry, "Back in the Saddle Again"

122 Dave Franklin, "Anniversary Waltz"

123 "Go Tell Aunt Rhody" (traditional)

124 "Yankee Doodle" (traditional)

125 Rudi Revil and John Turner, "The Little Shoemaker"

126 Mahler, Symphony No. 1, first movement

pp   sehr zart

127 Jule Styne, "Make Someone Happy"

f

128 Bartók, No. 16 from *44 Duets*, vol. I (adapted)
Repeat the melody and sing it as a canon with a partner. When the first singer begins m. 2,
the second begins m. 1.

p   sf

129 Irving Berlin, "Always"

mp

130 Bartók, No. 9 from *44 Duets*, vol. I (adapted)

f

131 Kurt Weill and Maxwell Anderson, "September Song"

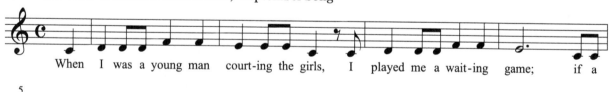

When I was a young man court-ing the girls, I played me a wait-ing game; if a

maid re-fused me with toss-ing curls, I let the old earth take a cou-ple of whirls,

132 John R. Cash, "I Walk the Line"
The anacrusis consists of three quarter notes.

I keep the ends out for the tie that binds._____ Be - cause you're mine _____

_____ I walk the line._____

133 José Padilla, "El Relicario"
The anacrusis consists of three eighth notes.

134 Bartók, No. 2 from *44 Duets*, vol. I (adapted)

135 Geoffrey Parsons, "Eternally"

136 Ted Daffan, "Born to Lose"

137 Bartók, No. 27 from *44 Duets*, vol. II

138 Clara Schumann, *Trois Romances*, Op. 11, No. 3 (adapted)

139 Wolfgang Amadeus Mozart, Piano Sonata in G Major, K. 283, second movement (adapted)

140 Pete Seeger, "Turn! Turn! Turn! (To Everything There Is a Season)"

141 Dave Loggins, "Please Come to Boston"

Hey ram - blin' boy,__ now won't you set-tle down   Bos-ton ain't your kind of town__ There

ain't no   gold__ and there ain't no - bod-y like   me_____

142 "Lil' Liza Jane" (traditional)

143 Ted Fiorito, "Charley, My Boy"

144 Bartók, No. 14 from *44 Duets*, vol. I

145 "Auld Lang Syne" (traditional)

146 Jack Sigler Jr., "Love (Can Make You Happy)"

147 Burton Lane, "Look to the Rainbow"

148 "Riddle Song" (traditional)

I gave my love a cher-ry that had no ___ stone. I gave my love a chick-en that had no ___ bone. I

gave my love a ring ___ with no end - ing. I gave my love a ba-by with no cry - ing.

149 "How Can I Keep from Singing?" (traditional)

150 George W. Meyer, "Where Did Robinson Crusoe Go with Friday on Saturday Night?"

151 "Every Time I Feel the Spirit" (traditional)

Sing mm. 1–16. After m. 16, return to the beginning (*da capo*, or *D. C.*) and sing until the first note in m. 8 (*Fine*).

Ensemble Melodies

Throughout the book there will be opportunities to perform in ensembles. Prepare each part separately, as for a single-line melody. Practice separately or in combination the rhythm, conducting, pitch, solfège syllables or scale-degree numbers, and musicality. If a part is too high or too low for your voice range, transpose it down or up an octave so it will be in a more comfortable register.

SUGGESTIONS FOR CLASS PERFORMANCE

- Choose an ensemble—one performer for each part.
- Choose a conductor, who will provide the tonic pitch and establish the tempo. Then every performer should conduct, following the conductor's lead.
- Stand while singing in order to produce the best sound.
- Maintain eye contact with each performer.
- Balance your part with the others.

VARIATIONS

- Switch parts and perform again until each musician has sung every part.
- Choose ensembles that feature more than one performer on each part.
- One musician can play one part while singing another.
- One musician can perform the rhythm of two parts simultaneously—tapping with each hand on a different surface or tapping one part while performing another vocally.

152 Ludwig van Beethoven, Gloria, from *Mass in C*, Op. 86

Pitches notated on a treble clef with an "8" beneath it sound one octave lower than written.

153 Beethoven, *German Dance* No. 11 (adapted)

154   Joseph Haydn, String Quartet in G Major, Op. 3, No. 3, third movement (adapted)

155   Beethoven, *German Dance* No. 2 (adapted)

156   Haydn, Piano Sonata No. 19 in D Major, third movement (adapted)

B. Major and Minor Keys, Simple and Compound Meters (Chapters 4–5)

C minor scale forms

Use the two charts below to learn the notes of the minor scale. When you can sing it comfortably, you are ready to sing the minor melodies that follow.

1. Begin by improvising melodies that consist only of pitches from the minor pentachord (written as whole notes).

2. When you have mastered the pentachord, add *ti* ($\hat{7}$) below and *le* ($\flat\hat{6}$) above. This embellished pentachord contains all the pitches of harmonic minor. Note that *ti* ($\hat{7}$) leads up to *do* ($\hat{1}$), while *le* ($\flat\hat{6}$) falls down to *sol* ($\hat{5}$).

3. Next, practice the upper tetrachords. When ascending from *sol* ($\hat{5}$), move to *do* ($\hat{1}$) through *la* ($\hat{6}$) and *ti* ($\hat{7}$); when descending from *do* ($\hat{1}$), fall through *te* ($\flat\hat{7}$) and *le* ($\flat\hat{6}$). The ascending melodic minor scale features the ascending tetrachord; the natural (descending melodic) minor scale features the descending tetrachord.

Embellished C minor pentachord (harmonic minor)

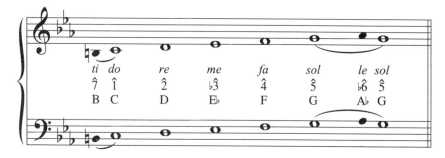

Upper tetrachords of the C minor scale

184

185

186

187

188

189

190

Part I Elements of Music

C minor pentatonic scale

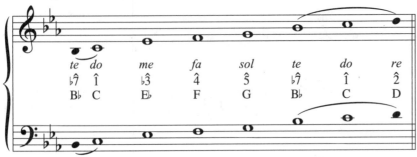

Music from the Literature

227   Joseph Haydn, String Quartet in G Minor, Op. 74, No. 3, second movement

228   Sergei Rachmaninov, Piano Concerto No. 3 in D Minor, first movement

229   George Philipp Telemann, Quartet in E Minor, third movement

230   Charles Gounod, "Où voulez-vous aller?" ("Where Do You Want to Go?") (adapted)

231   Clara Schumann, *Caprice à la Boléro* (adapted)

232   "Ah, Poor Bird" (traditional; round in three parts)

233   Ludwig van Beethoven, Agnus Dei, from *Mass in C*, Op. 86

234   William Billings, "Babylon" (round in three parts)

235   Johann Sebastian Bach, Sonata No. 1 in B Minor for flute and harpsichord, third
movement (adapted)

236   Arthur Sullivan, "I am the captain of the *Pinafore*" (adapted), from *H.M.S. Pinafore*

237   Beethoven, String Quartet in A Minor, Op. 132, fifth movement (adapted)

238   Clara Schumann, Variation 6 from *Variations on a Theme by Robert Schumann*

239   Franz Schubert, "Der Jäger" ("The Hunter"), from *Die schöne Müllerin*

240   Beethoven, Cello Sonata in A Major, Op. 69, second movement (adapted)

241 Alexander Glazunov, "Volga Boat Song," from *Symphonic Poem*, Op. 13

242 Aaron Copland, Piano Concerto, second movement

243 Bach, *Violin Partita No. 1* in B Minor, Bourrée

244 Johannes Brahms, *Intermezzo* in A Minor, Op. 116, No. 2

245 Beethoven, Sonatina in G Major, second movement (Romanze)

246 Philip Adair, "Arizze"

247 Beethoven, *German Dance* (adapted)

248 George Gershwin and DuBose Heyward, "Summertime," from *Porgy and Bess*

Your ___ dad-dy's rich ___ and your mam-ma's good look - in'

___ so hush lit - tle ba - by don't ___ you cry. ___

249 Béla Bartók, from *Hungarian Sketches* No. 1 (adapted)

250 "Geneva" (Protestant hymn, traditional) This melody begins in minor and changes to the parallel major.

251 Philip P. Bliss, "Wonderful Words of Life"

252 "Niño precioso" ("Precious Baby") (traditional)

253 Fanny Mendelssohn Hensel, "Schwanenlied" ("Swan Song") (adapted)

254 Schubert, "Venetianisches Gondellied" ("Song of a Venetian Gondolier")

255 Bach, *Violin Partita No. 1* in B Minor, Sarabande

256 Gabriel Fauré, *Elégie*, Op. 24, for cello and orchestra

Ensemble Melodies

257   Haydn, Piano Sonata No. 15 in C Major, first movement

258   Haydn, Piano Sonata No. 14 in D Major, second movement

259   Henry Purcell, *Minuet* (adapted)

260   Wolfgang Amadeus Mozart, *Exsultate, jubilate*, third movement
Remember that F♯ is called *di* (♯1̂).

261 Orlando Gibbons, "O Lord, Increase My Faith"

C. Major and Minor Keys, Simple and Compound Meters, Beat Subdivisions (Chapters 6–8)

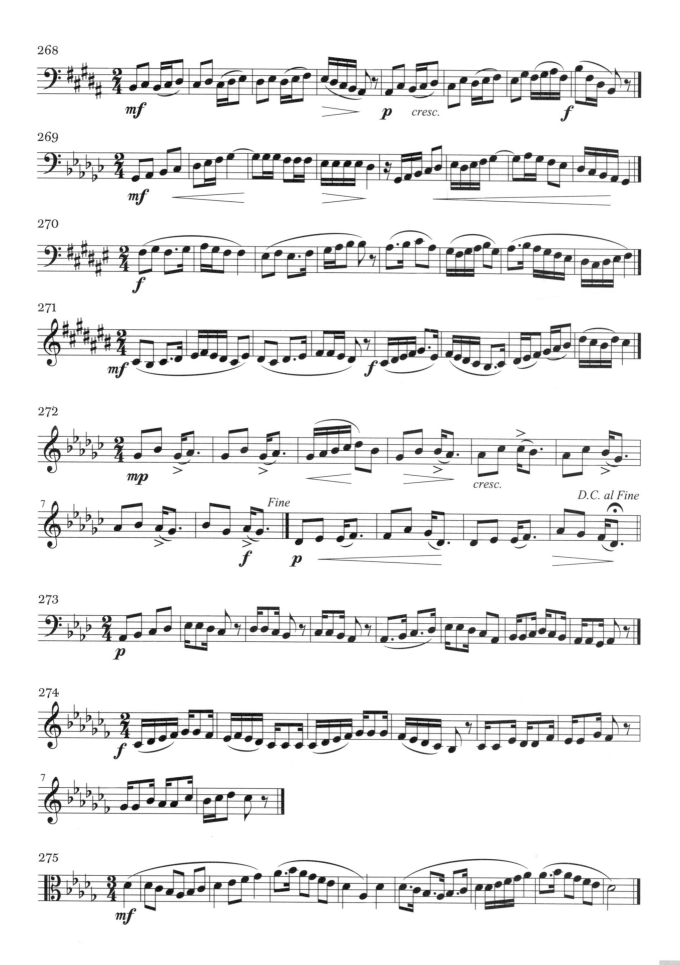

327 Minor-key fifths

328 Major-key sixths

329 Minor-key sixths

330 Major-key sevenths

331 Minor-key sevenths

332 Major-key triads étude

333 Minor-key triads étude

334 Major-key seventh chords

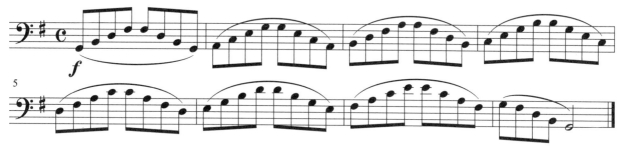

335 Minor-key seventh chords

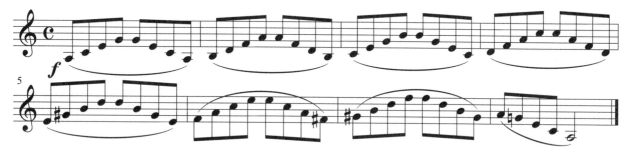

336 Seventh chords étude

337 Seventh chords étude

Music from the Literature

338 Wolfgang Amadeus Mozart, Piano Sonata in D Major, K. 284, third movement (adapted)

339 Clara Schumann, *Le Ballet des Revenants* (adapted)

340 Francesca Caccini, "Maria, dolce Maria" (adapted)

341 Johann Sebastian Bach, Violin Concerto No. 1 in A Minor, first movement

342 Gustav Mahler, Symphony No. 1, third movement

343 Johannes Brahms, *Intermezzo* in C♯ Minor, Op. 117, No. 3 (adapted)

344 Bach, Aria, from the *Anna Magdalena Bach Notebook*

345 Frédéric Chopin, Cello Sonata in G Minor, Op. 65, first movement

346 Bach, *Passacaglia* in C Minor for organ

347 "Jingle Bells" (traditional)

348 "Dubinushka" ("Hammer Song") (traditional)

349 Scott Joplin, "Ragtime Dance"

350 Frank Churchill, "Little April Flower"

351 "St. James Infirmary" (anonymous)

352 V. Solovyev-Sedoy, "Moscow Nights"

353 Bach, *Art of the Fugue*, Contrapunctus I

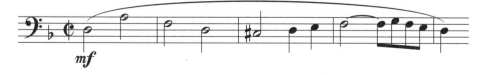

354 Jacques Offenbach, "Infernal Galop," from *Orphée aux enfers* (adapted)

355 Chopin, Cello Sonata in G Minor, Op. 65, third movement

356 Bach, *Musette* (adapted)

357 Franz Schubert, "Hirtenlied" ("Shepherd's Song")

358 Peter Ilyich Tchaikovsky, "Old French Song"

359   "Oh, Danny Boy" (traditional)

360   Clara Schumann, Piano Trio in G Minor, Op. 17, first movement

361   Claude Debussy, "Passepied," from *Suite bergamasque* (adapted)

362   Frances Flores del Campo, "Mi caballo blanco" ("My White Horse")

363 "Wade in the Water" (African American spiritual)

Perform in four, then again as if the melody were notated in cut time.

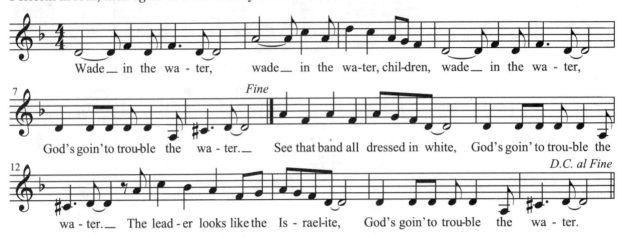

Wade__ in the wa - ter, wade__ in the wa-ter, chil-dren, wade__ in the wa - ter,

God's goin' to trou-ble the wa - ter.__ See that band all dressed in white, God's goin' to trou-ble the

wa - ter.__ The lead - er looks like the Is - rael-ite, God's goin' to trou-ble the wa - ter.

364 Bach, Fugue in G Minor for organ, BWV 535

365 Bach, Fugue in G Minor, from *The Well-Tempered Clavier*, Book I

366 Schubert, *Moment Musical*, Op. 94, No. 3

This excerpt concludes on the tonic.

367 Edvard Grieg, *Album Leaf*, Op. 12, No. 7

368 Joseph Haydn, String Quartet in F Minor, Op. 20 No. 5, first movement

369   Garry Bonner and Alan Gordon, "Happy Together"

Im-ag-ine me and you,___ I do,   I think a-bout you day and night,___ it's on-ly

right,   to think a-bout the girl you love,___ and hold her tight, so hap-py to - geth-er.___

370   "Gaudeamus Igitur" (traditional)

371   "The Maids of the Mourne Shore" (traditional)

372   Felix Mendelssohn, "Wenn sich zwei Herzen scheiden" ("When Two Hearts Must Part")

373   Brahms, "Spanisches Lied" ("Spanish Song"), Op. 6
Practice by filling in skips with pitches from the prevailing scale.

374 Clara Schumann, *Romanze*
The melody begins on *me* (♭3̂).

375 Mozart, String Quartet No. 3 in G Major, K. 156, second movement

376 Robert Schumann, "Knight Rupert," from *Album for the Young*, Op. 68, No. 12

377 John Lennon and Paul McCartney, "Let It Be"

When I   find my-self ___ in times of trou-ble   Moth-er Mar - y comes to me

Speak-ing words of wis - dom,   Let it be ___   and in my hour of dark - ness She is

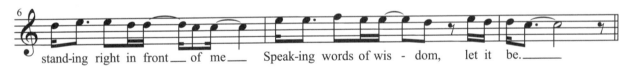

stand-ing right in front ___ of me ___   Speak-ing words of wis - dom,   let it be. ___

378 Clara Schumann, *Drei Romanzen*, Op. 21, No. 1
This melody begins on *sol* (5̂).

379 Brahms, *Intermezzo* in A Minor, Op. 76, No. 7 (adapted)

380 Beethoven, Piano Sonata in A♭ Major, Op. 110, Fugue (adapted)

381 Bach, Violin Concerto No. 1 in A Minor, third movement (adapted)

382 "Hunting Call" (traditional)

383 "The Haymaker's Jig" (traditional)

384 "The Butterfly" (traditional)

385 "Smash the Windows" (traditional)

386 "The New-Married Couple" (traditional)

387 Louise Farrenc, Trio in E Minor for flute, cello, and piano, Op. 45, first movement (adapted)

388 Mendelssohn, "Andres Maienlied" ("Another May Song"), Op. 8, No. 8

389 Mozart, Piano Sonata in G Major, K. 283, third movement (adapted)

390 Bach, No. 48 from *St. John Passion*

391 Alan Price, "The House of the Rising Sun"

There is ___ a house in New Or-leans, _____ they call ___ the Ris - ing Sun. _____ and it's

been ___ the ruin ___ of man-y a poor boy, _____ and God, ___ I know ___ I'm one. ___

392 Ottorino Respighi, *Lauda per la Natività del Signore (Praise for the Savior's Birth)* (adapted)

393 George Frideric Handel, *Harpsichord Suite in G Major*, Gigue

394 Schubert, "Frühlingstraum" ("Dream of Spring"), from *Winterreise*

395 Leopold Mozart, *Minuet* (adapted)

396 Mahler, Symphony No. 2, fifth movement (adapted)

397 Anton Bruckner, Symphony No. 4, fourth movement

398   Mahler, Symphony No. 2, fifth movement (adapted)

399   Grieg, *Waltz*, Op. 12, No. 2

400   Debussy, "Le Faune," from *Fétes galantes*, Book 2 (adapted)

401   H. Worthington Loomis, "The Frog in the Bog" (round in three parts)

402   Brahms, Double Concerto in A Minor, Op. 102, first movement (adapted)

Ensemble Melodies (Chapters 9–10)

403   Daniel Gottlob Turk, "The Hunters" (adapted)

404   "Who Stole My Chickens?" (traditional)

405   Mahler, Symphony No. 1, third movement

406   Haydn, String Quartet in F Major, Op. 3, No. 5, second movement (adapted)

407   François Couperin, *Les Moissonneurs* (adapted)

408 Haydn, String Quartet in D Minor, Op. 42, first movement (adapted)

409 Thomas Morley, "April Is in My Mistress' Face"

A-pril is in my Mistress' face,   A-pril is in my Mis-tress' face, my

A-pril is in my Mis   -   tress' face,   A-pril is in my Mis - tress'

A-pril is in my Mis   -   tress'

A-pril is in my Mis-tress' face,

Mis - tress' face,   A-pril is in my Mis-tress' face, And Ju-ly in her eyes   hath place,

face,   A-pril is in my Mis-tress' face, And Ju-ly in her eyes   hath place,

face, A-pril is in my Mis-tress' face, my Mis-tress' face,

A-pril is in my Mis-tress' face, my Mis-tress' face,

410 Robert Schumann, String Quartet in A Major, Op. 41, No. 3, fourth movement (adapted)

411 Haydn, String Quartet in G Major, Op. 3, No. 3, first movement

412 Beethoven, *German Dance* No. 10 (adapted)

413 Henry Purcell, "What Shall I Do"

414 Thomas Weelkes, "Lady, Your Eye My Love Enforced"

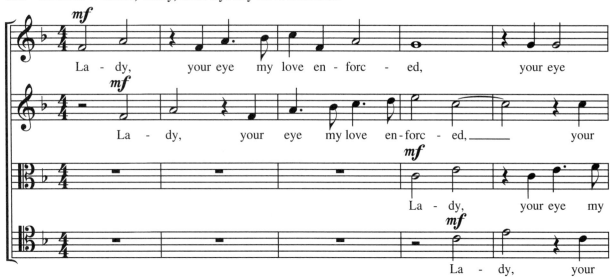

415 Mozart, Piano Sonata in A Major, K. 331, third movement (Rondo *alla Turca*)

416 Handel, *Suite in D Minor* (G. 121), Gigue (adapted)

417 "Man Is for the Woman Made" (adapted)

Sing mm. 1–8 in four parts; add a fifth part in m. 9.

418 David Arkin and Earl Robinson, "Black and White"

A child is black, a child is white, to - geth-er they grow ___ to

see the light, _____ to see the light. _____

419 Johann Christian Bach, Sonata in C Minor, Op. 17, No. 2

420 Smokey Robinson, "You've Really Got a Hold on Me"

You've real-ly got a hold on me. _____ You've real-ly got a hold __ on me.

You've real-ly got a hold on me. _____ You've

real - ly got a hold on __ me. real - ly got a hold on __ me.

D. Modal Melodies (Chapters 5ff.)

Melodies 421–440 feature the white-key modes, which may be transposed and notated with key signatures, accidentals, or both, as is demonstrated in the melodies from the literature. Review this section at the beginning of Part IV, as many twentieth-century composers draw on modes in their works.

Two singing methods are possible. In method 1, the final (tonic) is always called *do* ($\hat{1}$). This method helps you relate the sounds of modes to the more familiar sounds of major and minor keys; helps with dictation, since you hear the mode's final as the work's centric pitch, analogous to a tonic; and helps you associate specific melodic patterns with solfège syllables and scale-degree numbers. For example, *do-mi-sol* ($\hat{1}$–$\hat{3}$–$\hat{5}$) represents the tonic triad in every major key as well as the first triad in every Mixolydian and Lydian mode. The disadvantage of this method is that it requires chromatic syllables, instead of the easier diatonic syllables.

In method 2, modal solfège and numbers always correspond to the same-key-signature major scale. This method is sometimes easier for sight-reading. Its chief disadvantage is that it does not reinforce pattern recognition across all keys and modes. For example, if we hear D–F–A in D minor, we sing *do-me-sol* ($\hat{1}$–$\flat\hat{3}$–$\hat{5}$), but the same pitches in D Dorian will be called *re-fa-la* ($\hat{2}$–$\hat{4}$–$\hat{6}$) and in D Phrygian *mi-sol-ti* ($\hat{3}$–$\hat{5}$–$\hat{7}$). Calling the same sound by different names can be confusing.

Dorian

Aeolian

Phrygian

Mixolydian

Lydian

Plainsong (Plainchant) Melodies

Medieval Roman Catholic liturgical music, called plainsong or plainchant, or simply chant, was monophonic and modal. Because the original form of chant notation is now archaic, this music is transcribed so that contemporary musicians may perform it more easily. Melismas (two or more pitches sung to a single syllable of text) are indicated with a slur between notes or by beaming notes together. Text phrase endings are marked with a short line through the top staff line or with a bar line. Syllabic emphasis is indicated by placing an acute accent symbol (´) over a vowel. The melodies are sung somewhat freely in rhythm, with modern rhythmic values indicating "short" or "long" more than precise rhythms.

441 *Veni creator Spiritus* (anonymous plainsong)

442 *Pange lingua* (anonymous plainsong)

443 *Salve Regina* (anonymous plainsong)

444 Antiphon for Vespers (anonymous plainsong), from *Liber usualis*

More Music from the Literature

445 "She Moved Through the Fair" (traditional)

My__ young love said to me__ my moth-er won't mind_____ and my fa - ther_

__ won't slight you for your lack of kind,_____ and she laid_____ her hand__ on

me and did say:_____ It____ will not be long, love,__ till our wed-ding day.___

446 "Old Joe Clark" (traditional)

Old Joe Clark had a house fif-teen sto-ries high and ev'-ry sto-ry

in that house was filled with chick-en pie! Fare thee well, Old Joe Clark,

fare thee well, I say; fare thee well, Old Joe Clark, I best be on my way.

447 Béla Bartók, *Hungarian Folk Song*

448 George and Ira Gershwin, "Oh, Lord, I'm on My Way," from *Porgy and Bess*

O, Lord,__ I'm on my way.__ I'm on my way__ to a heav'n-ly land.__

449 Joe Satriani, "Flying in a Blue Dream"

450 "Canoeing Song" (traditional)

451 Antonin Dvořák, Symphony No. 5 in E Minor, fourth movement

452 Bartók, No. 18 from *44 Duets*, vol. I (adapted)

453 Bartók, No. 37 from *44 Duets*, vol. II (adapted)

454 "Cumberland Nelly" (traditional)
The melody concludes on its final, E.

455 John Logan, "Consolation," from *Sixteen Tune Settings* (1812)

456 "Hey, Ho, Anybody Home?" (traditional; round in three parts)

Hey, ho, an - y - bod - y home? Meat nor drink nor mon - ey have I none. Yet will I be mer - - - ry!

457 "Shalom, Chaverim" ("Peace, Friends") (traditional; round in three parts)

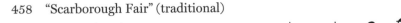

458 "Scarborough Fair" (traditional)

Are you go-ing to Scar-bo-rough fair? ___ Pars-ley, sage, rose - mar-y, and thyme. ___ Re-mem-ber me to one who lives there. ___ S/he was once a true love of mine. ___

459 "Dance of Youth" (traditional)

The final of this mode is D.

460 Bartók, No. 6 from *44 Duets*, vol. I (adapted)

The final of this mode is E.

461 "Land of the Silver Birch" (traditional)

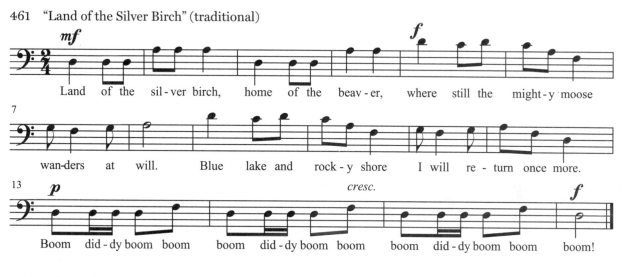

462 "The Bird Song" (traditional)

Ensemble Melodies

463 Bartók, No. 39 from *44 Duets*, vol. II (adapted)

464 Giovanni Pierluigi da Palestrina, *Alleluia tulerunt Dominum,* first three entrances
Assume G to be the final. Sing *te* (♭$\hat{7}$) for the pitch F.

465 Orlande de Lassus, *Expectatio justorum laetitia*

Rhythm-Reading

When performing rhythms, always set a tempo *before* beginning; if a tempo is not indicated, set a comfortable one for yourself that you can maintain for the entire exercise. Practice with the tempo *already* set before you begin. Also:

- Keep time while you perform the rhythms by conducting or tapping lightly.
- Sing the rhythm with counting syllables as indicated by your instructor, or on a neutral syllable such as "da" or "ta."
- Perform the rhythms *musically*, with attention to dynamics, phrasing, and relative stress of stronger and weaker beats.
- The duets can be performed with a partner; by tapping the lower part with the left hand and the upper part with the right; by playing on the keyboard with two different notes; or by singing one part while tapping/playing the other.

A. Simple Meters (Chapters 2–3)

When conducting duple meter, your arms should move throughout each beat. Use large gestures, and make a small bounce, called the ictus, on each beat number. Practice in pairs in class, conducting while facing each other. Or practice alone before a mirror until your gestures look natural and your arms move on "autopilot." Variation: Conduct with both hands, the left mirroring the motion of the right to improve the coordination in your nondominant hand.

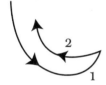

Simple duple

Perform each rhythm while tapping or conducting in two with a steady beat. Follow the dynamics indicated, and perform with an inflected tone—that is, one that indicates a clear sensitivity to phrasing and the relative strength of beats. Variation: Choose your own pitches on which to perform the rhythms. Sing with solfège syllables, scale-degree numbers, or letter names. Start with two pitches, e.g., *do–mi* ($\hat{1}$–$\hat{3}$), and gradually add more.

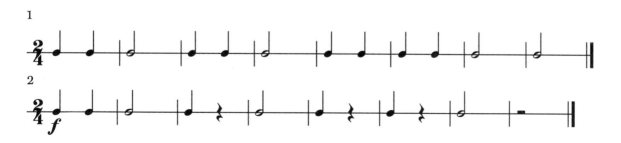

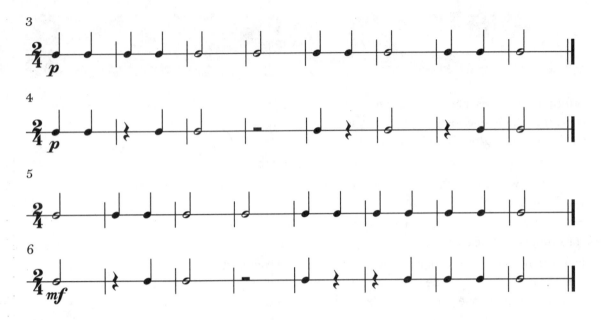

Some of the next rhythms begin with an anacrusis, the value of which is subtracted from the final measure. Prepare to perform by counting silently one full measure plus one beat. Perform aloud beginning with the anacrusis, moving *toward* the downbeat, and continue with a steady tempo until the end.

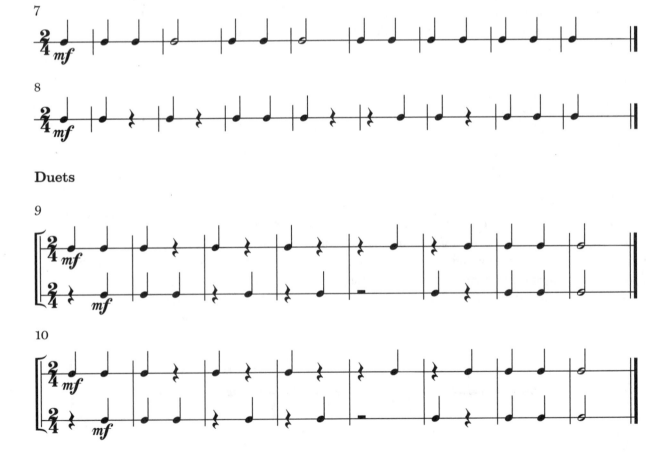

Duets

Simple quadruple

Following the downbeat in quadruple meter, beat 2 crosses the chest, beat 3 swings back out to the side, and beat 4 is an upbeat.

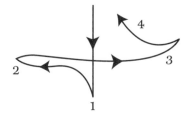

RHYTHM PATTERNS: o DURATION

1. Point to a numbered rhythm pattern below and perform it. Keeping a steady beat, point to a new pattern and perform it. Continue in this way until you have performed five patterns. Optional: Read each pattern with counting syllables recommended by your instructor.

2. Ties, dots, and syncopation: Perform examples (a), (b), and (c) to learn how to change patterns 4, 5, and 3 into three new patterns.

(a) Pattern 4   + tie   = pattern 6

(b) Pattern 5   + tie   = pattern 7

(c) Pattern 3   + tie   = pattern 8 (syncopation)

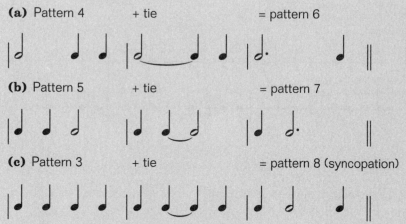

3. Improvise phrases drawn from all eight patterns. Variation: Have a classmate point to patterns, in any order, while you perform. Switch roles.

11

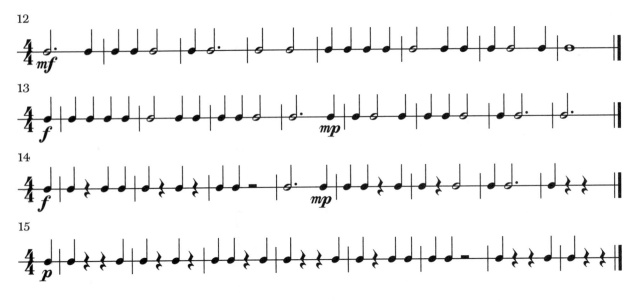

Duets

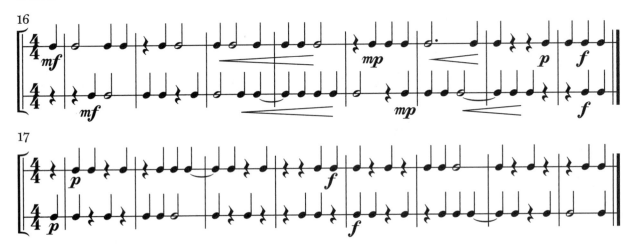

Simple triple

In triple meter, after conducting the downbeat, move your arms out to the side for beat 2.
The third beat is an upbeat again.

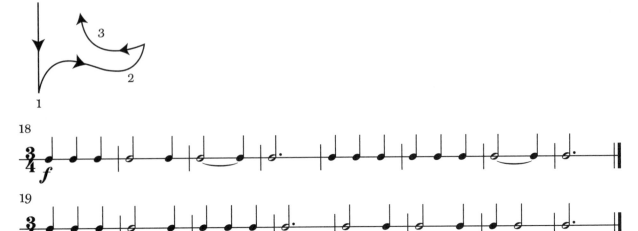

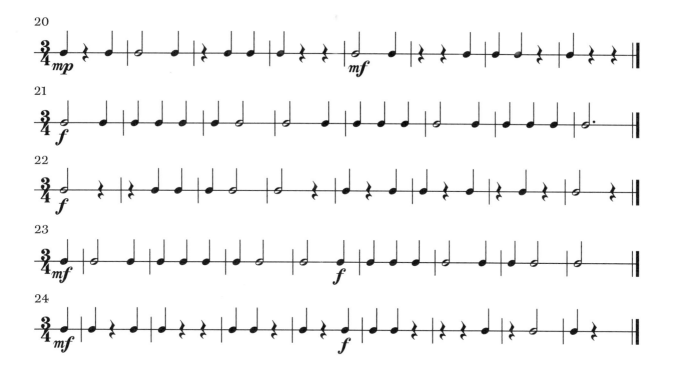

Duet

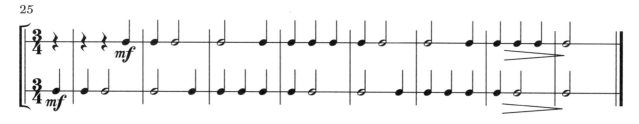

RHYTHM PATTERNS: ♩ BEAT UNIT

1. Basic patterns

2. Ties, dots, and syncopation

(a) #4   + tie   = #6   **(b)** #5   + tie   = #7   **(c)** #3   + tie   = #8

3. Complete patterns

Simple duple

Simple quadruple

Duets

Simple triple

Duets

55

5

56

5

RHYTHM PATTERNS: 𝅝 BEAT UNIT

In cut time and $\frac{2}{2}$ meter, the half note is the beat unit; the two quarters are the beat division.

1. Patterns

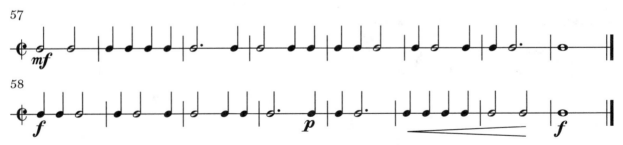

2. Improvise phrases drawn from the new list of patterns above. Variation: Have a classmate point to patterns, in any order, while you perform. Switch roles.

Simple duple

57

58

The following rhythm is performed exactly like the one above.

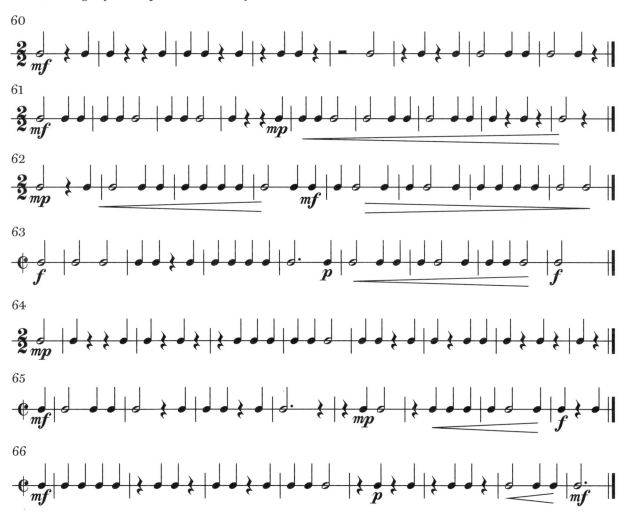

Duets

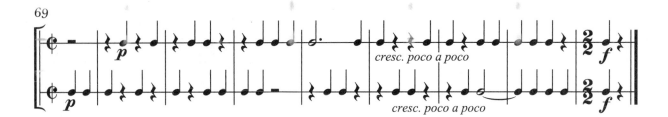

Simple quadruple

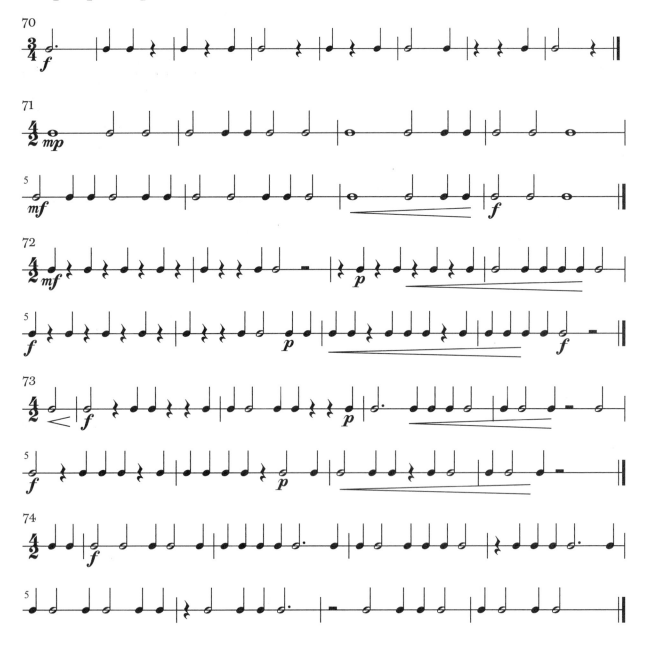

Duets

Simple triple

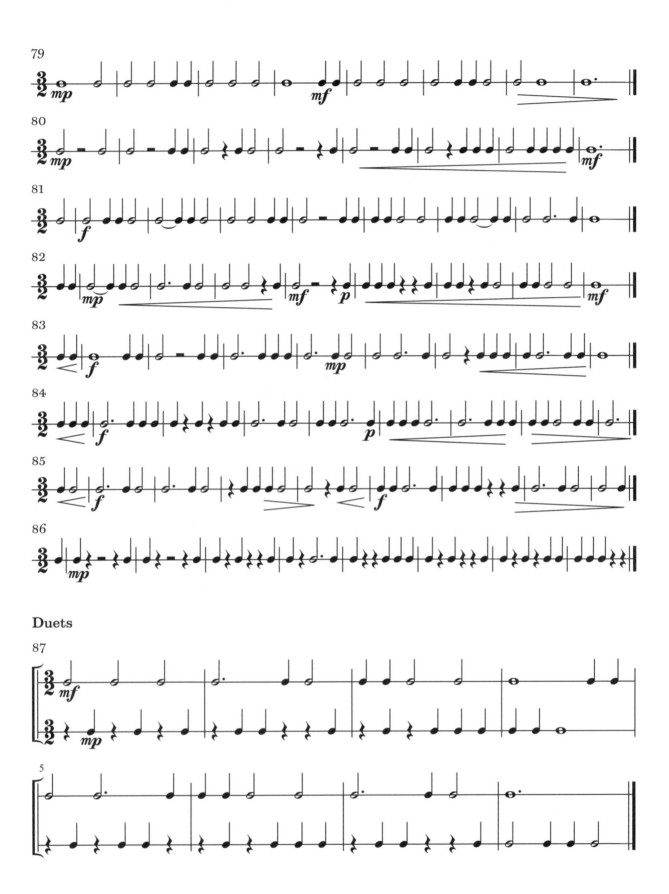

Duets

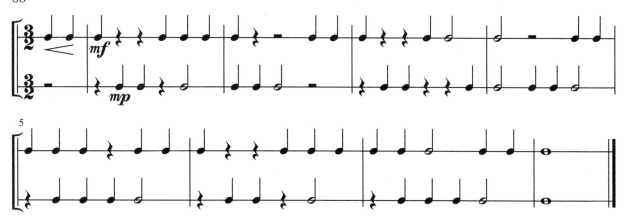

B. Compound Meters (Chapter 4)

RHYTHM PATTERNS: ♩. BEAT UNIT

In compound meters, the dotted note gets one beat that divides into three parts. Perform these exercises following the procedures given on page 81.

Tying two dotted-quarter notes produces a dotted half, which fills an entire measure in this compound-duple meter.

Compound duple

92

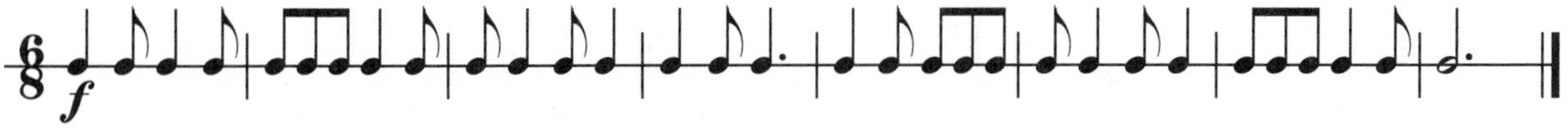

93

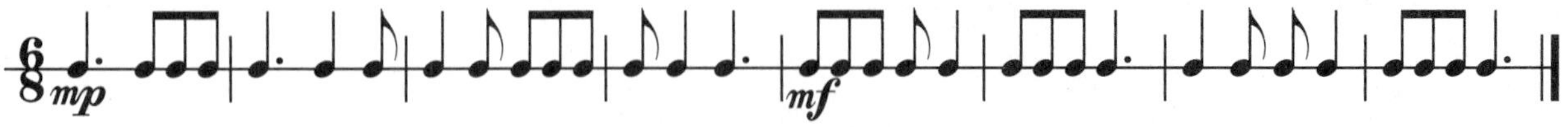

94

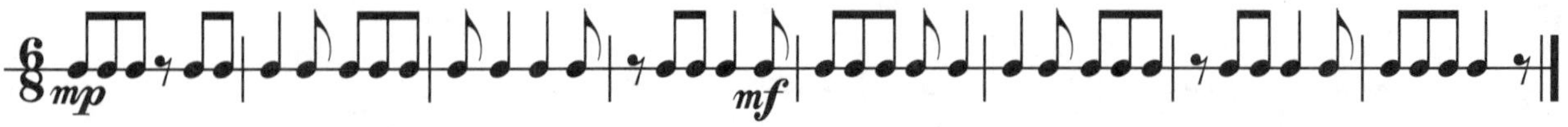

95

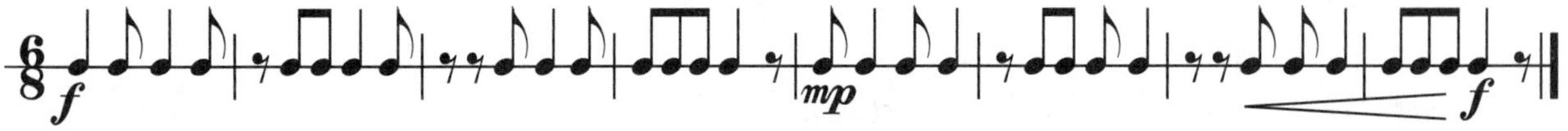

96

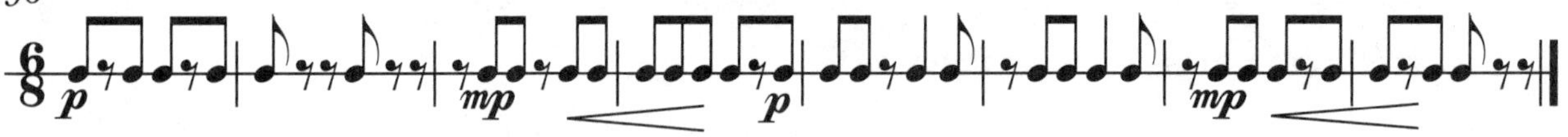

97

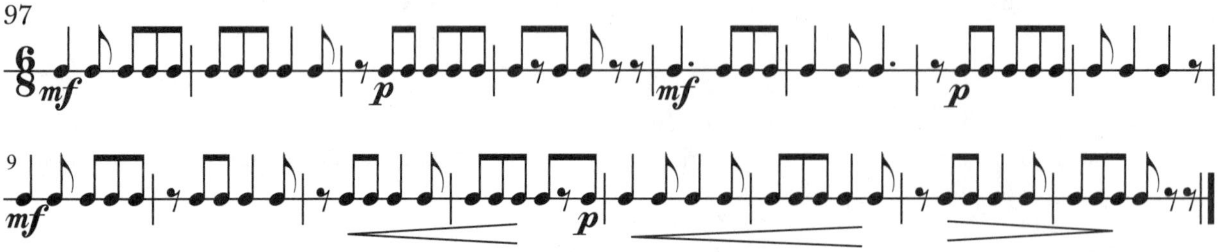

98

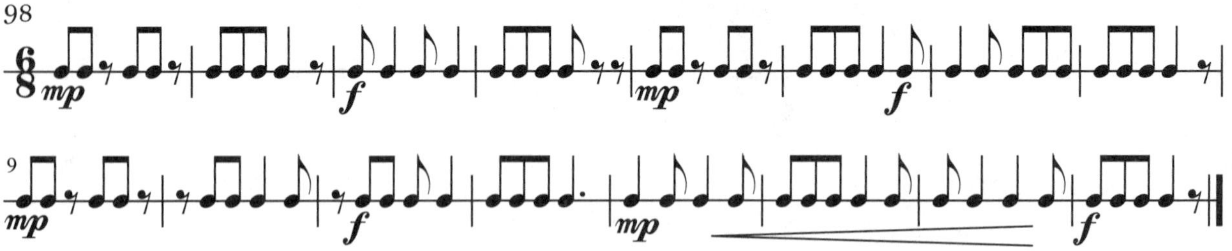

99

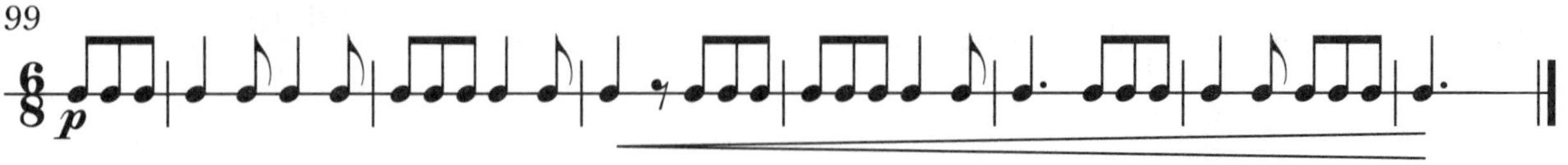

100

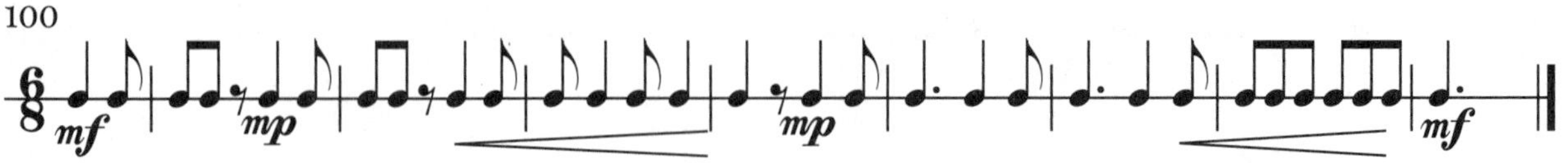

Compound quadruple

Duets

113

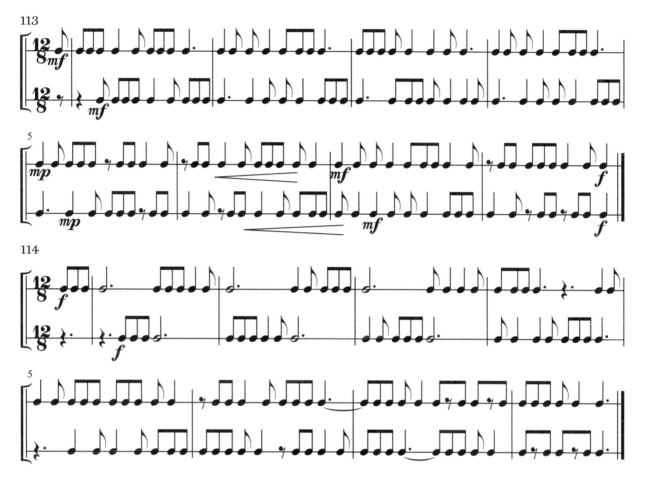

Compound triple

115

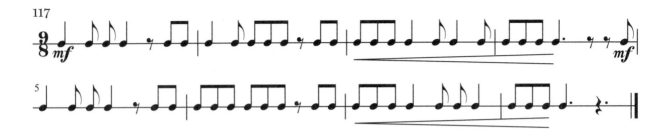

The next rhythms begin with anacruses of various durations, the value of each one subtracted from the final measure. Count silently two or three beats, imagining the three-part division of each beat. Perform aloud beginning with the anacrusis, moving *toward* the downbeat, and continue with a steady tempo until the end.

Duets

♩. beat unit: Compound duple

Duet

127

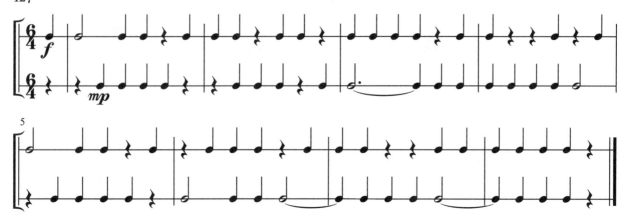

Compound quadruple

128

129

130

Duet

131

Compound triple

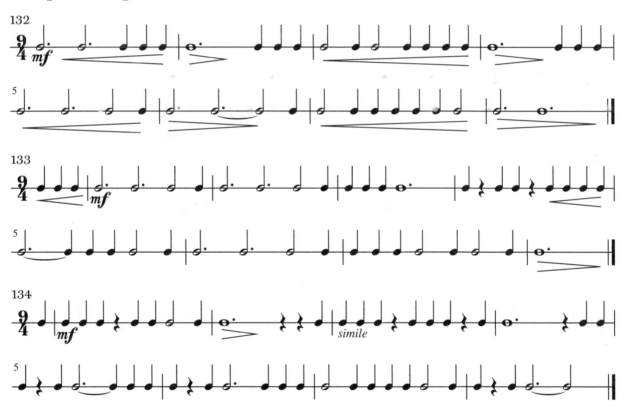

Duet

135

C. Simple Meters with Beat Subdivisions (Chapters 5–6)

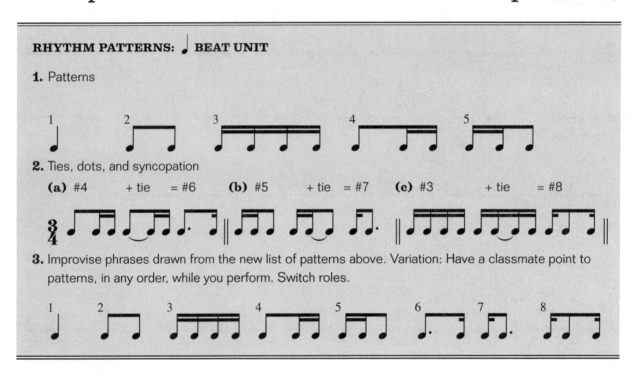

RHYTHM PATTERNS: ♩ **BEAT UNIT**

1. Patterns

2. Ties, dots, and syncopation

(a) #4   + tie   = #6   **(b)** #5   + tie   = #7   **(c)** #3   + tie   = #8

3. Improvise phrases drawn from the new list of patterns above. Variation: Have a classmate point to patterns, in any order, while you perform. Switch roles.

Simple duple

136

137

Duets

Simple quadruple

Duets

Simple triple

Duets

♩ beat unit: Simple duple

The next rhythms begin with a quarter-note anacrusis.

Simple quadruple

Duet

Simple triple

Duets

D. Compound Meters with Beat Subdivisions (Chapters 7–8)

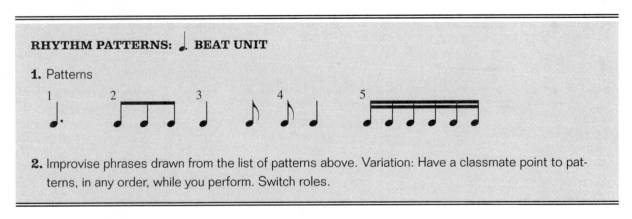

RHYTHM PATTERNS: ♩. **BEAT UNIT**

1. Patterns

2. Improvise phrases drawn from the list of patterns above. Variation: Have a classmate point to patterns, in any order, while you perform. Switch roles.

Compound duple

The next five rhythms show how a tie within the beat can be added to one pattern in order to create a new one.

Duets

Compound quadruple

204

Duets

205

206

Compound triple

211

♩. beat unit: Compound duple

213

214

215

Duets

216

217

Compound quadruple

218

Duet

Compound triple

E. Borrowed Beat Divisions ("Tuplets") (Chapters 9–10)

Duets

Simple meter with 𝅗𝅥 beat unit

243

Duets

248

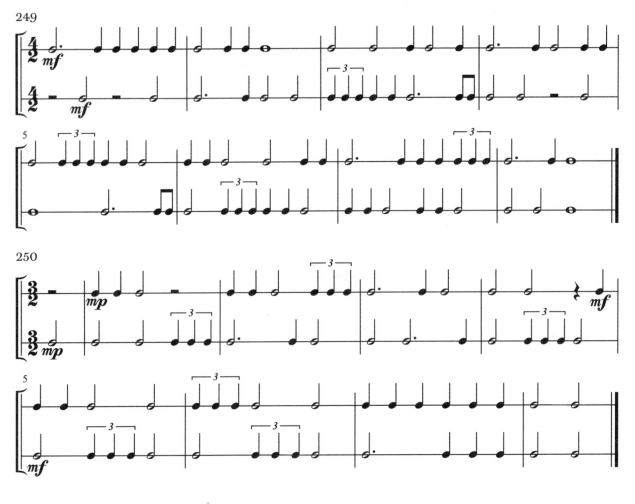

Compound meter with ♩. beat unit

Duets

263

Compound meter with 𝅗𝅥. beat unit

264

265

266

267

268

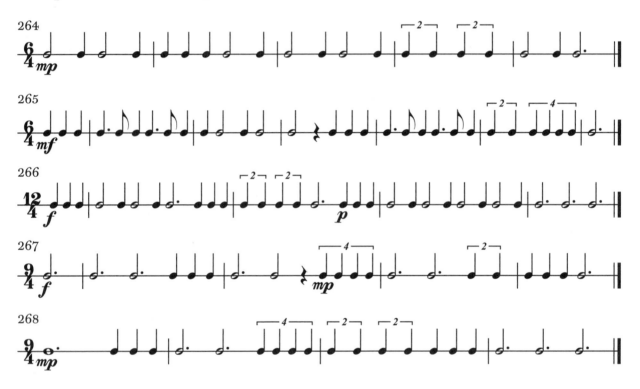

Duets

269

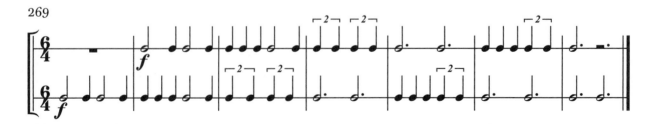

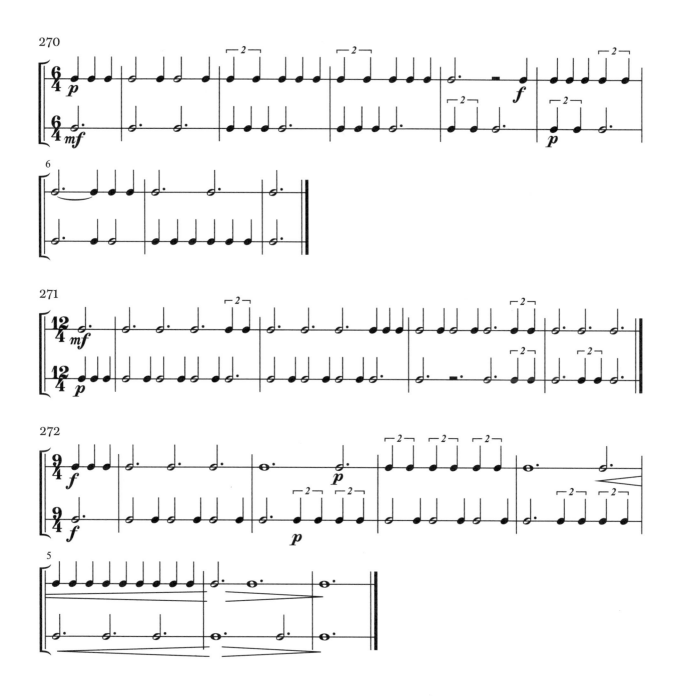

Diatonic Harmony
and Tonicization

Sight-Singing

A. Phrases (Chapters 11–13)

Half- and dotted-half-note beat unit

466   William Byrd, Galliarde to the First Pavian (adapted), from *My Lady Nevell's Book*

467   Byrd, "Ye Souldiers Dance," from *My Lady Nevell's Book*

468   Thomas J. Williams, "Ebenezer" (Protestant hymn melody, 1890)

Ensemble Melodies

469   Byrd, Galliarde to the Sixte Pavian, from *My Lady Nevell's Book*

470 John Dowland, "Now, O Now I Needs Must Part"

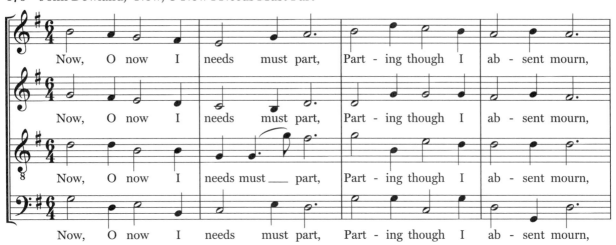

Now, O now I needs must part, Part - ing though I ab - sent mourn,

Now, O now I needs must part, Part - ing though I ab - sent mourn,

Now, O now I needs must part, Part - ing though I ab - sent mourn,

Now, O now I needs must part, Part - ing though I ab - sent mourn,

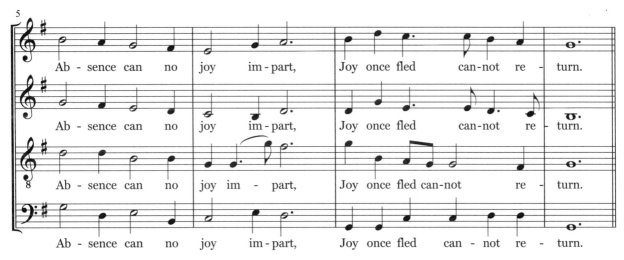

Ab - sence can no joy im - part, Joy once fled can-not re - turn.

Ab - sence can no joy im - part, Joy once fled can-not re - turn.

Ab - sence can no joy im - part, Joy once fled can-not re - turn.

Ab - sence can no joy im - part, Joy once fled can-not re - turn.

471 Barbara Strozzi, "Dessistete omni, pensiere," from *Ariette a voce solo*, Op. 6

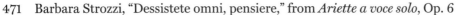

472 William Byrd, "The Carman's Whistle," *My Lady Nevell's Book*

Outer voices in eighteenth-century style

Chapter 11 demonstrates how two-part counterpoint is related to the outer voices typical of eighteenth-century music. To help you understand the counterpoint, write interval numbers between the staves. Sing one part while playing the other, then switch. Perform these melodies in class as duets or ensembles.

473 Johann Sebastian Bach, "O Ewigkeit, du Donnerwort" ("O Eternity, Word of Thunder"), BMV 60

In m. 4, C♯ is *si* (♯5̂).

474 Bach, "Was Gott tut, das ist wohlgetan" ("What God Does Is Well Done"), BMV 99

475 Bach, "Jesu, der du meine Seele" ("Jesus, Who Saved My Soul"), BMV 78

476 Bach, "Nun komm, der Heiden Heiland" ("Now Come, Savior of the Gentiles"), BMV 61

In m. 5, hear *ti* (7̂, A♯) in relation to *do* (1̂).

477 Bach, "Wer nur den lieben Gott lässt walten" ("He Lets Only Beloved God Rule"), BMV 93

In m. 3, tune *te* (♭7̂) by imagining *do* (1̂) during the quarter rest.

478 Bach, "Erhalt uns, Herr, bei deinem Wort" ("Preserve Us, God, by Your Word"), BMV 126

479 Bach, "Ich freue mich in dir" ("I Rejoice in You"), BMV 133

480 Joseph Haydn, String Quartet in E♭ Major, Op. 33, No. 2 (*The Joke*), third movement (adapted)

481 Haydn, String Quartet in F Major, Op. 20, No. 5, third movement (adapted)

482 Isabella Leonarda, Credo, from *Messa Prima*

This excerpt is actually two-part music. Because the upper parts have the same rhythm and contour, they act as a single part that counterpoints the bass. To analyze the intervals, first compare the highest part with the bass, then the middle part with the bass.

Harmonic progressions

Sing these études to learn the sound of T–D–T progressions. Stems-down pitches represent the bass lines; listen especially to these notes or have a partner sustain them while you sing the melody. Sing the melodies in their parallel keys, too.

483 I–V⁶–I

484 I–V$^6_5$–I

485 I–V$^4_3$–I^6

486 I–V$^4_2$–I^6

487 I–V7–I

488 Getting the most out of this étude:

- Play the bass line while singing the melody with solfège syllables and scale-degree numbers.

- Have a partner sing the bass line while you sing the treble part.

- To realize the progression in block chords at the keyboard, hold the three highest treble pitches and play the bass line.

- Play the four-part progression in block chords while singing the melody as notated.

Conclusive and inconclusive cadences

For conclusive cadences: Listen for the cadential melodic pitch to be *do* ($\hat{1}$). For inconclusive cadences: Listen especially for pitches such as *re* ($\hat{2}$), *ti* ($\hat{7}$), or *sol* ($\hat{5}$); less conclusive cadences might end with *mi* ($\hat{3}$).

489 James Horner and Will Jennings, "My Heart Will Go On," from *Titanic* (adapted)

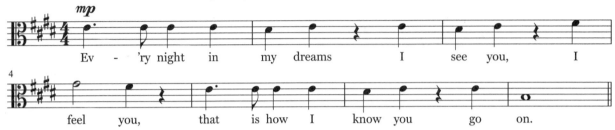

Ev - 'ry night in my dreams I see you, I

feel you, that is how I know you go on.

490 Gustav Mahler, Symphony No. 2, first movement (adapted)

491 Edvard Grieg, *Norwegian Melodies*, Op. 63, first movement
(This melody is in a minor key.)

492 Gale Garnett, "We'll Sing in the Sunshine"

We'll sing in the sun - shine, _____ We'll laugh ev - 'ry day; _____

we'll sing in the sun - shine _____ and I'll be on my way. _____

493 Frédéric Chopin, Cello Sonata in G Minor, Op. 65, first movement

494 Al Kasha and Joel Hirschhorn, "Candle on the Water"

I'll be your can-dle on the wa - ter, My love for you will al-ways burn. I know you're

lost and drift-ing, but the clouds are lift-ing, don't give up, you have some-where to turn.

495 John Denver, Bill Danoff, and Taffy Nivert, "Take Me Home, Country Roads"

Al - most heav - en __ West Vir - gin - ia __

Blue Ridge Moun - tains, __ Shen - an - do - ah Riv - er. __

496 Redd Stewart and Pee Wee King, "Tennessee Waltz"

I was waltz - ing __ with my dar - lin' __ to the Ten - nes - see __

Waltz __ when an old friend I hap - pened to see. __

497 Haydn, String Quartet in G Minor, Op. 74 No. 3, second movement

498 Franz Liszt, *Hungarian Rhapsody* No. 14

499 Bach, No. 48 from *St. John Passion*

500 James Taylor, "Carolina on My Mind"

Kar - lin she's __ a sil - ver sun, __ you'd best walk her a - way and

watch it shine. Watch her watch __ the morn - ing come. __

501 Bruce Johnston, "I Write the Songs"

I write the songs _ that make the whole world sing; I write the songs _ of love and spe - cial things. __ I write the songs _ that make the young girls cry; __ I write the songs, I write the songs. __

502 Giambatista Martini, *Gavotte in F*

503 Johnny Marks, "Silver and Gold" (adapted)

Sil - ver and gold, sil - ver and gold, ev' - ry-one wish-es for sil - ver and gold.

504 Hank Cochran, "Make the World Go Away"

Do you re-mem-ber when you loved me be-fore the world took me a - stray? If you do, then for - give me, and make the world _ go a - way.

505 John Denver, "Annie's Song"

D   G   A   Bm   G   D

You fill up my sen - ses ___ like a night in a for-est. ___

506 Mahler, Symphony No. 2, second movement

507 Bach, *Partita No. 3* in A Minor, BMV 827, Burlesca

508 Franz Schubert, "Das Wandern" ("Wandering"), from *Die schöne Müllerin*

Ensemble Melodies

509 Muzio Clementi, Sonatina in C Major, Op. 36, No. 1, third movement (adapted)

Play one part and sing the other, or perform as a duet.

510 Georg Philipp Telemann, *Fantaisie* in E Minor (adapted)

511 Bach, *Suite No. 2* for orchestra, BWV 1067, from Badinerie

512 Stephen Foster, "Better Times Are Coming"

Play the piano part and sing the other, or perform as a quintet.

There are voic - es of hope that are borne on the air, and our land will be freed from its clouds of des-pair, for brave men and true men to bat - tle have gone, and good times, good times are now com - ing on.

513 Bach, Duet 2 from *Clavierübung III* (adapted)

514 Haydn, String Quartet in D Major, Op. 50, No. 6, first movement

Sing the tonic pitch, then find *re* (2̂), the starting pitch.

515 Haydn, String Quartet in G Minor, Op. 20, No. 3, first movement

A passing V$^4_3$ is implied in m. 1, but because the viola doubles violin 1, the *do–ti–do* (1̂–7̂–1̂) line is not present.

B. Embellishing Phrases (Chapters 14–17)

Mixed beat divisions

Before singing the next group of melodies, prepare by establishing the meter's simple beat division, then alternate between simple and compound divisions as notated. Listen to phrase endings and decide if a cadence is conclusive, less conclusive, or inconclusive. Then identify the specific type of cadence: PAC, IAC, or HC.

516 Franz Liszt, *Hungarian Rhapsody* No. 15

517 Gustav Mahler, Symphony No. 2, fifth movement

518 Ernest Chausson, "Les Papillons," Op. 2, No. 3

poco rit.

519 Frédéric Chopin, Nocturne in G Minor, Op. 37, No. 1

520 Al Lewis, Vincent Stock, and Larry Rose. "Blueberry Hill"

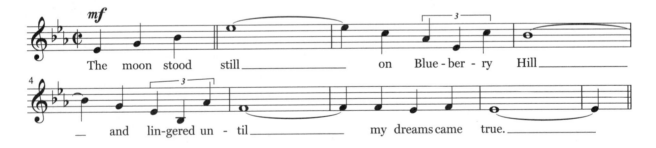

The moon stood still_____ on Blue-ber-ry Hill_____

___ and lin-gered un-til_____ my dreams came true._____

Ensemble Melodies

521 Joseph Haydn, Piano Sonata No. 18 in B♭ Major, second movement (adapted)

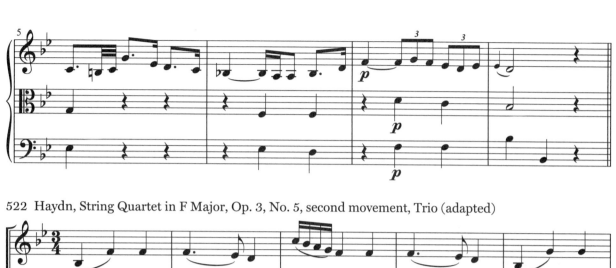

522 Haydn, String Quartet in F Major, Op. 3, No. 5, second movement, Trio (adapted)

523 Maciej Radziwill, *Polonaise* (adapted)

Tapping the eighth notes will help you perform the triplet correctly. Sing the treble part
while playing the bass, or perform as a trio.

More embellishing tones

The next group of melodies emphasize the motivic use of neighbor tones. Look for them
to be diatonic or chromatic, complete or incomplete, single or double.

524 Jerome Kern, "The Song Is You"

525 Irving Berlin, "White Christmas"

526 John Hill Hewitt, "All Quiet Along the Potomac To-night"

Tune *fi* (♯$\hat{4}$) in m. 14 by hearing its resolution to *sol* ($\hat{5}$) in m. 15 as part of a double neighbor figure.

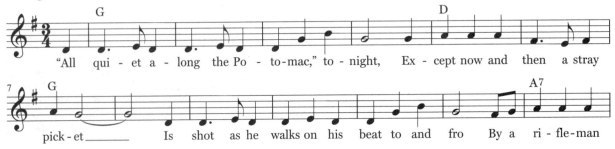

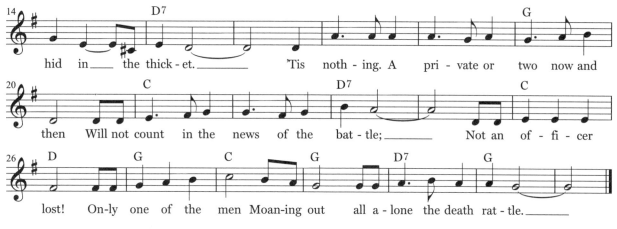

hid in___ the thick - et._____ 'Tis noth - ing. A pri - vate or two now and
then Will not count in the news of the bat - tle;_____ Not an of - fi - cer
lost! On-ly one of the men Moan-ing out all a - lone the death rat - tle._____

527 "Morrison's Jig" (traditional)

Modes can have conclusive and inconclusive cadences, too.

528 Bert Kaempfert, "Strangers in the Night"

529 Felix Mendelssohn, *Song Without Words*, Op. 62, No. 4 (adapted)

530 Gene Lees and Amando Manzanero, "Yesterday I Heard the Rain"

Yes - ter - day I heard the rain, whis - per - ing your name,
(echo)
ask - ing where you'd gone. It fell soft - ly from the clouds
(echo)
on the si - lent crowds as I wan-dered on.

531 Richard Rodgers and Lorenz Hart, "Bewitched"

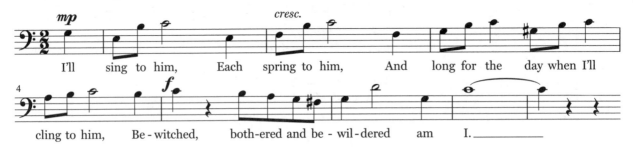

I'll sing to him, Each spring to him, And long for the day when I'll

cling to him, Be - witched, both-ered and be - wil - dered am I._____

The rhythm of the next four melodies should be "swung"—that is, the beat should be divided long-short, similar to compound meter's ♩ ♪ rhythm.

532 Horace Silver, "The Preacher"

He would stand up there in the pul - pit, horn in his hand,__ and

let that mel - o - dy take__ you to the Prom - ised Land.__

533 Frank Perkins, "Stars Fell on Alabama"

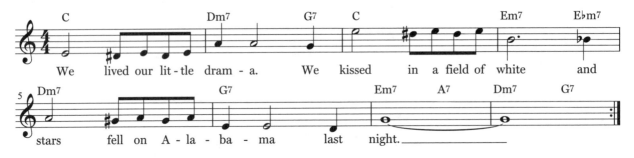

We lived our lit - tle dram - a. We kissed in a field of white and

stars fell on A - la - ba - ma last night._____

534 Sammy Cahn and Jule Styne, "It's Been a Long, Long Time"

This dotted notation was often featured in mid-twentieth-century melodies to indicate that the rhythm should be swung.

Just kiss me once, then kiss me twice, then kiss me once a - gain, it's been a

long, long time. Have - n't felt like this, my dear, since

can't re - mem - ber when, it's been a long, long time.

535 Ted Koehle and Harold Arlen, "Stormy Weather"

Some slow jazz pieces are notated in cut time because there is a two-beat feel in the accompaniment. You may perform this melody as if it were notated in common time, with a ♩ beat circa 60.

Don't know why_____ there's no sun up in the sky, Storm-y Weath-er,_____

Since my man and I __ ain't to-geth-er,_____ keeps rain-in' all __ the time._____

536 Ned Washington and Leigh Harline, "When You Wish Upon a Star"

If your heart is in your dream, no re - quest is too ex - treme,

When You Wish Up - on A Star as dream - ers do.

537 Andrew Lloyd Webber, Charles Hart, and Richard Stilgoe, "All I Ask of You" (adapted)

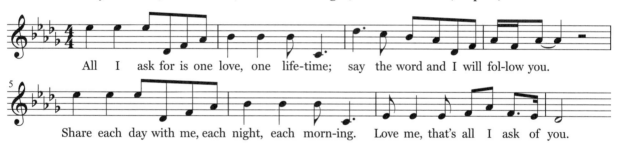

All I ask for is one love, one life-time; say the word and I will fol-low you.

Share each day with me, each night, each morn-ing. Love me, that's all I ask of you.

Improve your proficiency with syllables or numbers by practicing these melodies slowly, then increasing your speed.

538 Wolfgang Amadeus Mozart, String Quartet No. 2 in D Major, K. 155, first movement (adapted)

539 Mozart, Piano Sonata in D Major, K. 311, third movement (adapted)

540 Haydn, Piano Sonata No. 40 in G Major, third movement (adapted)

Ensemble Melodies

541 Haydn, Piano Sonata No. 15 in C Major, Menuetto

542 Ludwig van Beethoven, *Ecossaise* in G (adapted)

543 Béla Bartók, No. 39 from *44 Duets*, vol. II

Singing vii°⁷

The étude below (544) features the common progressions i–vii°7–i, i–vii°6–i⁶, and i–vii°⁴₃–i⁶. The vii°7 chord is often suggested by the outline of intervals d7 and A2, which are created by *ti* ($\hat{7}$) and *le* ($\flat\hat{6}$) in the harmonic minor scale.

- Sing with the accompaniment to help tune the chord, then without.
- Sing as a trio.
- Follow the melodic tendencies of vii°7's chord tones: *ti* ($\hat{7}$) leads to *do* ($\hat{1}$); *le* ($\flat\hat{6}$) falls to *sol* ($\hat{5}$); *fa* ($\hat{4}$) falls to *me* ($\flat\hat{3}$).
- Sing in the parallel major. Recall that the leading-tone seventh chord's quality is half-diminished (vii⌀7).

544

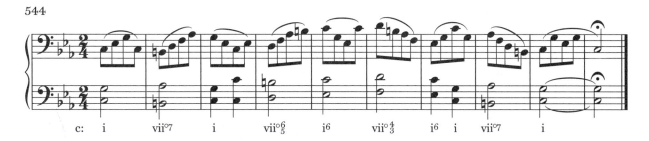

545 Johann Sebastian Bach, Fugue in C Minor, BMV 546

M. 3 outlines vii°7.

546 Bach, Invention No. 4 in D Minor

M. 2 outlines vii°7, which has been filled in with passing tones.

547 Beethoven, String Quartet in F Major, Op. 18, No. 1, second movement (adapted)

The arrows show vii°7, which is filled in with passing tones and embellished with a chromatic lower neighbor.

548 *Musical challenge!* Bach, Double I from *Violin Partita No. 1* in B Minor (adapted)

In m. 1, *ti* (7̂) and *le* (♭6̂) suggest vii°7. Follow the guide tones in the lower staff to help you perform this compound melody.

C. Phrase Organization (Chapters 18–19)

Harmonizing melodies

Develop a routine like the one below, and follow it each time you harmonize a melody.

- Harmonize melodies in keyboard style (three voices in the right hand, the bass voice in the left).
- Employ I$^{(6)}$, V$^{(6)}$, and all positions of the dominant seventh chord, as well as ii^6, IV, and V$^{6-5}_{4-3}$.
- Look for common two- and three-pitch melodic patterns that may be harmonized with the progressions you have learned. Model your voice-leading on these progressions.
- Experiment with the harmonic rhythm, changing chords once per bar, once per beat, or each time you change the pitch.
- Sing the melodies while you play your harmonization, or accompany a classmate's instrumental performance of the melody.
- Play slowly, but in rhythm, until you create a satisfying phrase.
- Direct the motion of each phrase to its cadence through the use of expressive devices, including dynamics.

For example, the first time you harmonize a melody, try an easy possibility, such as that shown in the first line beneath the staff. When you have mastered the easy version, try more challenging harmonizations, like the second line.

						V7				I	V	I
I	V	I		I	V$^4_3$	I^6	I	ii^6		V$^6_4$ —— $^8_6$ $^7_5$ ^{3}		I

549 Ludwig van Beethoven, Symphony No. 9 in D Minor, fourth movement (adapted)

550 Modest Musorgsky, "The Great Gate of Kiev," from *Pictures at an Exhibition* (adapted)

551 "Are You Sleeping?" (traditional)

552 Amy Beach, "Forgotten"

553 "We Three Kings" (traditional)

Harmonize phrase 1 in E minor and phrase 2 in G major, as indicated. Remember to raise
the leading tone in the dominant chord. At the end, try a plagal resolution.

e: G:

554 Johannes Brahms, Clarinet Quintet, Op. 115, third movement

555 Hugo Wolf, "Das verlassene Mägdlein" ("The Abandoned Maiden")

556 George Frideric Handel, *Suite in F Major* (G. 178), from Fugue

Try harmonizing the last two measures using ii⁶–V⁷–I. Could IV–V⁷–I work, too?

557 Joseph Haydn, String Quartet in D Major, Op. 33, No. 6, first movement

Try using a neighboring $^6_4$ in your harmonization of m. 1, and I⁶–V$^4_3$–I–V in m. 2.

558 "Amazing Grace" (traditional)

559 Dottie West, Bill Davis, and Dianne Whiles, "Country Sunshine"

I was raised on coun-try sun - shine, I'm hap-py with the sim-ple things, _ A
Sat-ur-day night dance, a pic-ture show,_ and the joy that the blue-bird brings. _

560 Haydn, String Quartet in E♭ Major, Op. 20, No. 1, second movement (adapted)

561 Roger Miller, "Oo-De-Lally"

562 "On the Erie Canal" (traditional); D Aeolian (or natural minor)

Try a Phrygian resolution in m. 2 and a deceptive cadence in m. 4.

563 Brahms, Symphony No. 3 in F Major, fourth movement (adapted)

Look closely at the key signature; end with a Phrygian cadence.

564 Beach, "Forgotten"

This was melody 552. Conclude with a Phrygian cadence.

565 Beach, "Barcarolle"

Each phrase may be harmonized with a plagal cadence.

Ensemble Melodies

Melodies 566–568 review PAC, HC, and Phrygian and plagal cadences.

566 Archangelo Corelli, *Sonata da Camera* in G Minor, Op. 4, No. 2, Corrente

Sing the violin parts down one octave.

567 Johann Sebastian Bach, "Jesu, meine Freude" ("Jesus, My Joy"), BWV 227 (adapted)

568 Orlando di Lasso, *Matona mia cara (My Dear Lady)*

For another example of a deceptive resolution, review melody 515.

Periods

569 This melody is based on Wolfgang Amadeus Mozart's Piano Sonata in D Major, K. 576, first movement.

570 Based on the traditional Shaker melody "Simple Gifts."

571 Based on Franz Schubert's "Des Müllers Blumen" ("The Miller's Flowers"), from *Die schöne Müllerin.*

572 Based on Felix Mendelssohn's "Spring Song," from *Songs Without Words*, Op. 62, No. 6.

573 "El Coqui" ("Little Frog") (traditional)

574 This étude will help you learn to improvise a parallel period. First sing line 1 to learn the melodic outline of each tune in lines 2–5. Sing parts 2–5 as individual melodic lines, or improvise a new variant of the melody by jumping from line to line on each measure or half-measure.

575 Tony Velona and Remo Capra, "O Bambino"

576 Elton John and Tim Rice, "Can You Feel the Love Tonight"

And can you feel＿ the love＿ to-night,＿ how it's laid＿ to rest?＿

It's e-nough＿ to make kings＿ and＿ vag-a-bonds＿ be-lieve the ver - y best.＿

577 Tom Blackburn and George Bruns, "Ballad of Davy Crockett"

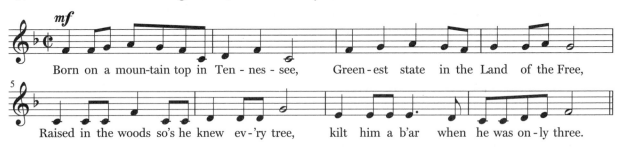

Born on a moun-tain top in Ten - nes - see, Green - est state in the Land of the Free,

Raised in the woods so's he knew ev -'ry tree, kilt him a b'ar when he was on - ly three.

578 Lionel Richie, "Three Times a Lady"

Thanks for the times that you've giv - en me.＿ The

mem-'ries＿ are all＿ in my mind.＿

Ensemble Melodies

579 Beethoven, *German Dance* No. 3

Sing *le* (♭$\hat{6}$) for D♭ and *fi* (♯$\hat{4}$) for B♮.

Part II Diatonic Harmony and Tonicization

580 Muzio Clementi, Sonatina in G Major, Op. 36, No. 5, Rondo

Play one part and sing the others, or perform as a trio.

Sequences

The following melodies feature melodic and/or harmonic sequences.

582 "Music Alone Shall Live" (traditional; canon in three parts)

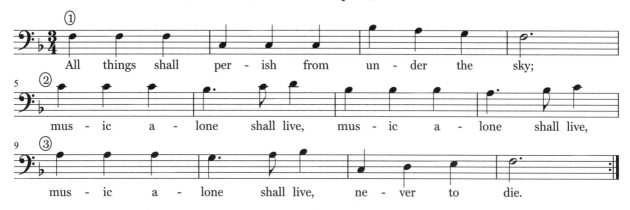

All things shall per - ish from un - der the sky;

mus - ic a - lone shall live, mus - ic a - lone shall live,

mus - ic a - lone shall live, ne - ver to die.

583 Elisabeth Jacquet de la Guerre, Chaconne, from *Pièces de Clavecin*

584 Fanny Mendelssohn Hensel, *Notturno* in G Minor

585 Jackie Rae and James Last, "Happy Heart" (adapted)

Mus - ic fills my soul___ now, I've lost all con - trol___ now,

I'm not half, I'm whole___ now with your love.___

586 Bach, Sonata II from *Six Trio Sonatas*, BWV 526

587 Manos Hadjidakis, "Never on a Sunday" (adapted)

Come an-y day and you'll be my guest, an-y day you

say, but my day of rest.

588 Amando Manzanero and Sid Wayne, "It's Impossible"

Can I hold you clos-er to me, and not feel you go-ing

through me, split the se-cond that I nev-er think of you? Oh, how im-

pos-si-ble.

589 Norman Gimbel and Charles Fox, "Happy Days"

Sun-day, Mon-day, Hap-py Days; Tues-day, Wednes-day, Hap-py Days,

Thurs-day, Fri-day, Hap-py Days; Sat-ur-day, What a day,

590 Jay Livingston and Ray Evans, "Mona Lisa"

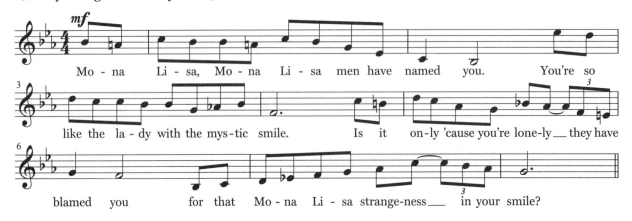

Mo-na Li-sa, Mo-na Li-sa men have named you. You're so

like the la-dy with the mys-tic smile. Is it on-ly 'cause you're lone-ly they have

blamed you for that Mo-na Li-sa strange-ness in your smile?

591 Haydn, String Quartet in E♭ Major, Op. 50, No. 3, first movement (adapted)

592 Schubert, Piano Sonata in G Major, Op. 147, third movement

593 Beethoven, Kyrie, from *Mass in C*, Op. 86

Ensemble Melodies

594 Haydn, String Quartet in E♭ Major, Op. 50, No. 3, fourth movement (adapted)

595 Haydn, String Quartet in E♭ Major, Op. 50, No. 3, second movement (adapted)

Discover the sequence type by determining the harmonic progression implied at the beginning of each phrase.

596 C. P. E. Bach, Sonata in F Major, W. 62/9 (adapted)

597 Haydn, Piano Sonata No. 33 in D Major, third movement (adapted)

598 Bach, Versus V from Cantata No. 4, *Christ lag in Todesbanden* (*Christ Lay in Death's Bonds*) (adapted)

599 Haydn, String Quartet in C Major, Op. 20, No. 2, third movement (adapted)

D. Tonicization (Chapters 20–21)

Harmonizing melodies with secondary-dominant-function chords

Sing each of the nine melodies that follow, then harmonize them. Sing again and accompany yourself with your harmonization. At places indicated with an arrow, use a secondary-dominant-function chord.

600 Peter Yarrow, "Puff, the Magic Dragon"

Here is a rare chance (in m. 2) to play the mediant triad, which is used when a melody falls through *ti* ($\hat{7}$).

601 Elisabeth Jacquet de la Guerre, "Air," from *Semelé*

602 Joseph Haydn, String Quartet in G Major, Op. 64, No. 4, third movement (violin 1 part)

603 Richard Rodgers, "People Will Say We're in Love," from *Oklahoma!*

604 Sarah Doudney, "The Ash Grove"

605 Johannes Brahms, *Liebeslieder Waltzer*, Op. 39, No. 15

606 Daniel Gottlob Turk, *Gavotte* (adapted)

Harmonize only mm. 1–8.

607 Franz Schubert, "Mit dem grünen Lautenband" ("With the Lute's Green Ribbon"),
from *Die schöne Müllerin*

608 Rodgers and Hammerstein, "Climb Ev'ry Mountain," from *The Sound of Music*

Climb   Ev' - ry   Moun-tain,   search   high   and   low,   Fol - low ev' - ry

by - way,   ev' - ry path   you know.

609 Mendelssohn, "Volkslied" ("Folk Song"), Op. 47, No. 4

610 Mendelssohn, "Lieblingsplätzchen" ("Favorite Place"), Op. 99, No. 3

611 Richard Strauss, "Für fünfzehn Pfennige" ("For Fifteen Pennies")

612 Mendelssohn, "Bei der Wiege" ("Beside the Cradle"), Op. 47, No. 6

613 Amy Beach, "Chanson d'Amour" ("Song of Love")

Note the duplets in compound meter. When harmonizing, tonicize V at the end.

614 Johann Sebastian Bach, Fugue in E Minor, from *The Well-Tempered Clavier*, Book II

Note the subtle relationship between the descending-line portion of the compound melody (beginning in m. 2, beat 4, with the equivalent durations of half notes: C–B–A–G–F♯s) and the same series of pitches in diminution (beginning in m. 5, beat 3: C–B–A–G–F♯s).

615 Frédéric Chopin, *Etude* in F Minor, Op. 10, No. 9

Sing this parallel double period in a comfortable range. Sing bracketed notes down one octave.

616 Fred Ebb and John Kander, "Willkommen," from *Cabaret*

Will - kom - men! Bien - ve - nue! Wel - come! im Cab - a -

ret, au Cab-a - ret, to Cab-a - ret! _____

617 James Rado, Gerome Ragni, and Galt MacDermot. "Where Do I Go?"

Yes - ter - day I heard the rain, whis - per - ing your name,

(echo)

ask - ing where you'd gone. It fell soft - ly from the clouds

(echo)

on the si - lent crowds as I wan-dered on.

618 Brahms, String Sextet No. 1 in B♭ Major, Rondo (cello part)

When harmonizing, try a deceptive resolution in m. 4 and V⁷/V at the cadence.

619 Mendelssohn, "Gruß" ("Greeting"), Op. 19, No. 5

620 Schubert, "Dankgesang an den Bach" ("Song of Thanks to the Brook"), from *Die schöne Müllerin*

621 John Lennon and Paul McCartney, "Yesterday"

Yes-ter-day ___ all my trou-bles seemed so far a - way. ___

Now it seems as though they're here to stay. ___ Oh, I be-lieve ___ in yes-ter-day. ___

622 Bart Howard, "Fly Me to the Moon"

Fly me to the moon, ___ and let me play a-mong the stars; ___

Let me see what spring ___ is like on Ju - pi-ter and Mars. ___

623 Mendelssohn, "Auf Flügeln des Gesanges" ("On the Wings of Song"), Op. 34, No. 2

624 Rodgers and Hammerstein, "It Might as Well Be Spring," from *State Fair*

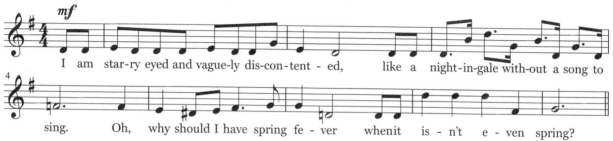

I am star-ry eyed and vague-ly dis-con-tent - ed, like a night-in-gale with-out a song to

sing. Oh, why should I have spring fe - ver when it is - n't e - ven spring?

625 Mendelssohn, "Frühlingslied" ("Spring Song"), Op. 79, No. 2

626 Dorothy Fields and Cy Coleman, "Sweet Charity"

Here was a man ___ with no dream and no plan ___ and one

lone - ly night I found ___ Sweet Char - i - ty. ___ You make life fun ___ for me,

oh, what it's done ___ for me, hav - ing you a - round. ___

627 Mendelssohn, "Wartend" ("Waiting"), Op. 9, No. 3 (adapted)

628 Carl Heinrich Carsten Reinecke, *Polka*

629 Fanny Mendelssohn Hensel, Song No. 3 from *Songs for Pianoforte*

Ensemble Melodies

630 Brahms, *Liebeslieder Waltzer*, Op. 52, No. 11

631 Ludwig van Beethoven, Piano Sonata in G Major, Op. 79, third movement

632 Giovanni Battista Pescetti, *Presto* (adapted)

633 Bach, "Herr Jesu Christ, dich zu uns wend" ("Lord Jesus Christ, Turn to Us"), from *Eighteen Chorale Preludes for Organ*, BWV 655 (adapted)

ground. Fa la la la la, fa la la la la la la la la la la la.

ground. Fa la la la la, fa la la la la fa la la la la la la.

ground. Fa la la la la, la la la la fa la la la la la la la la.

ground. Fa la la la la, fa la la la la la la.

ground. Fa la la la la la, fa la la la la, la la la la la la.

635 Bach, "Ich liebe Jesum alle Stund'" ("I Love Jesus in Every Hour")

636 Beethoven, *German Dance* No. 6, Minuet (adapted)

637 Beethoven, *German Dance* No. 6, Trio

638 Bach, "Nun lob', mein' Seel', den Herren" ("Now Praise, My Soul, the Lord"), BMV 390

From the anacrusis to m. 5 to beat 1 of m. 6, switch syllables or numbers to reflect the tonicization of vi.

639 Bach, *Suite No. 2* for orchestra, Bourrée II (adapted)

640 Henry Purcell, "Air" (adapted)

641 Bach, "Jesus Christus, unser Heiland" ("Jesus Christ, Our Savior"), from *Eighteen Chorale Preludes for Organ*, BWV 666 (adapted)

Sing the chorale (first line), then the prelude below to discover how Bach derives and develops his motive.

642 Bach, "Herr, wie du willst, so schicks mit mir" ("Lord, Deal with Me as You Wish"),
BMV 73

Look for raised pitches to act as leading tones to the scale degree they tonicize.

643 Bach, Duet 2 from *Clavierübung III*

644 Bach, Duet 3 from *Clavierübung III* (adapted)

Rhythm-Reading

A. Simple Meters:  Beat Units with Subdivisions

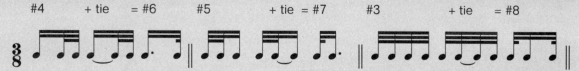

RHYTHM PATTERNS OF ♪ BEAT UNIT

1. Point to a numbered rhythm pattern below and perform it. While keeping a steady beat, point to a new pattern and perform it. Continue in this way until you have performed five patterns. Optional: Read each pattern with counting syllables recommended by your instructor.

2. Ties, dots, and syncopation: Perform the examples below to learn how to change rhythm patterns 4, 5, and 3 into three new patterns.

3. Create new rhythm compositions from the list of eight patterns below. Variation: Have a classmate point to patterns, in any order, while you perform. Switch roles.

♪ **beat unit**

273

Andante ("Walking" tempo)

274

275

Allegro (Cheerful, fast)

The next five exercises indicate a disruption in pulse, by means of a fermata (∩), which directs you to hold a note for longer than its established duration; a breath mark, or caesura (ʼ); or a general pause (grand pause, G.P.). As you conduct, practice not only how you begin the disruption, but how you return to the original pulse.

276

Maestoso (Majestically)

277

Andante

278

Adagio (Slow)

279

Adagio

280

Vivace (Lively)

281

Presto (Very fast)

289

Moderately

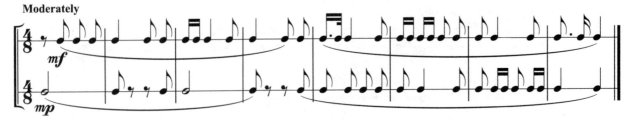

290

Allegro

291

Vivace

♩ **beat unit**

292

Vivo (Alive)

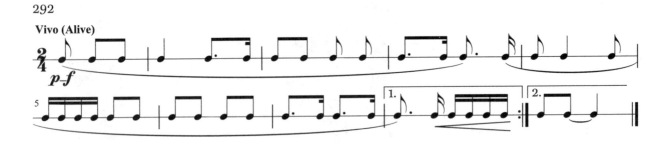

293

Andante

305

Slowly

306

Moderato

307

Andante

♩ **beat unit**

308

Allegro

309

Andante

310

Moderato

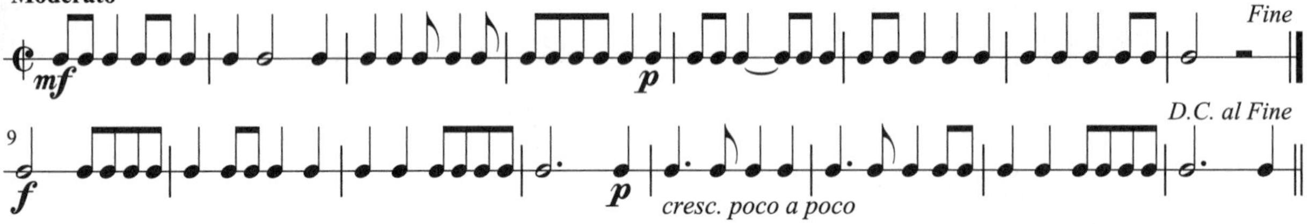

311

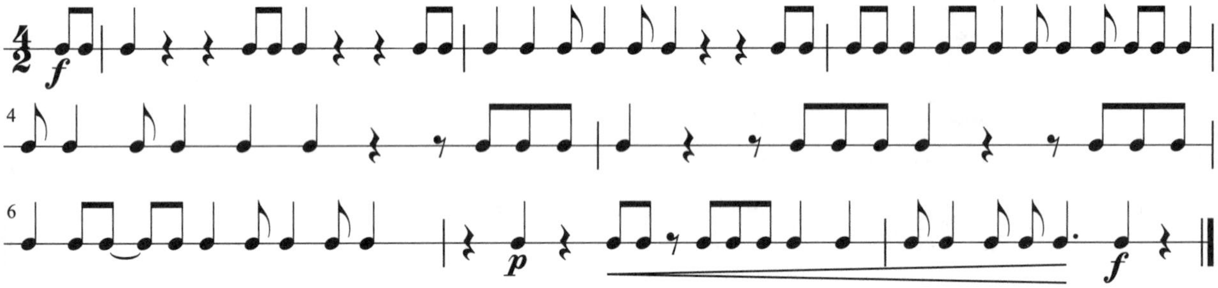

312

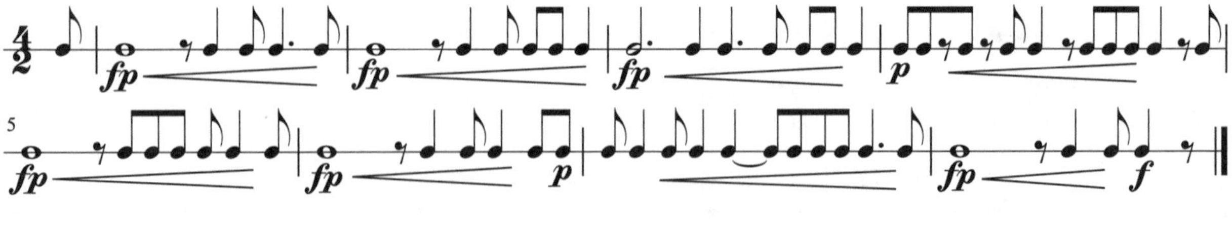

Duets

317

318

B. Compound Meters: ♪, ♩ and ♩. Beat Units with Subdivisions (Chapters 14–15)

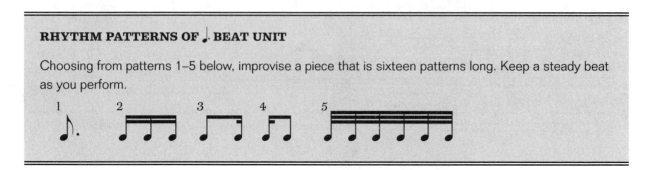

RHYTHM PATTERNS OF ♩. BEAT UNIT

Choosing from patterns 1–5 below, improvise a piece that is sixteen patterns long. Keep a steady beat as you perform.

♪. **beat unit**

Rhythms 319–324 appear in pairs—the first with ties, the second without.

329

330

331

♩. beat unit

332

333

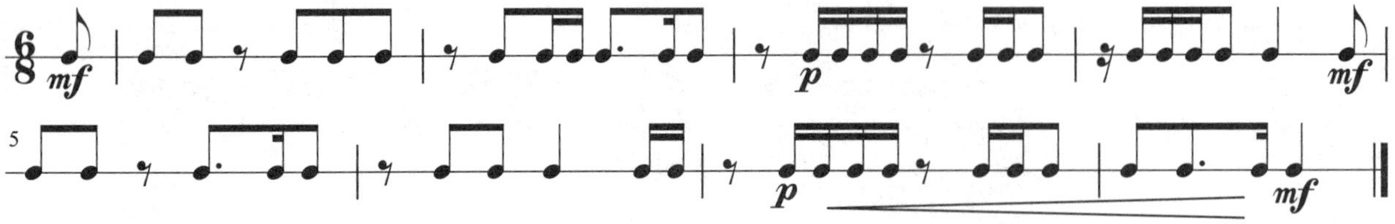

334

Animato (Animated)

335

Sostenuto (Sustained)

336

Alla marcia

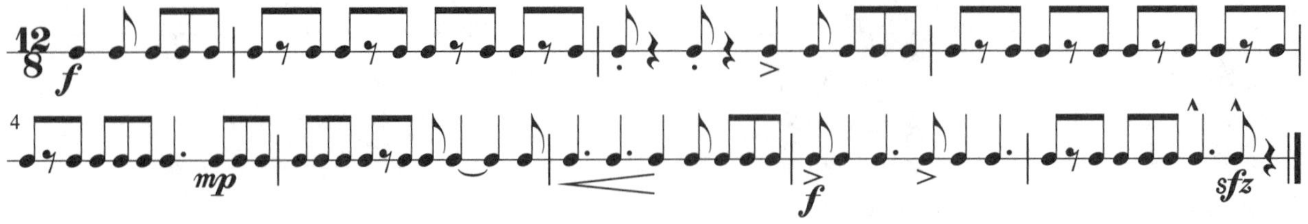

337

Briskly

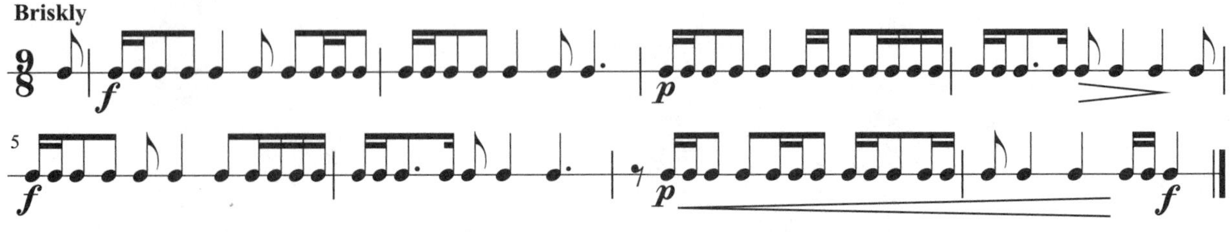

338

Calmly

339

340

Duets

341

♩. **beat unit**

345
Allegretto

346

347
Grazioso (Gracefully)

348

349

350

351

Largo (Slow)

352

Larghetto (Slightly faster than Largo)

Duets

353

Allegretto

354

355

C. Compound (Super) Triplets (Chapters 16–17)

The following rhythms include **compound triplets**, also called **super triplets**, three notes that occur in the space of two beats. To prepare, conduct rhythm 356 in two. In mm. 4–5, perform only the notes with stems up, while imagining the triplet division (stems down).

356

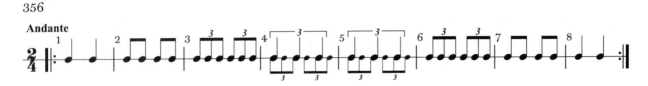

Now compare mm. 3, 6, and 7 in rhythm 357a with those in rhythm 357b. Rhythm 357a features true compound (super) triplets, which are always evenly spaced. Rhythm 357b includes an unequal pattern of sixteenth notes (3+3+2) that is often mistaken for compound triplets; these false triplets are called "Broadway," or "rumba," triplets.

Duets and Trio

366

367

368

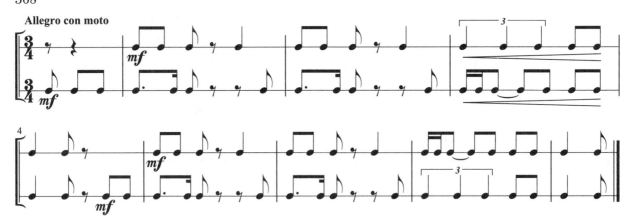

 beat unit

369

Part II Diatonic Harmony and Tonicization

370

Largo (Slow)

371

Alla marcia

372

Lento

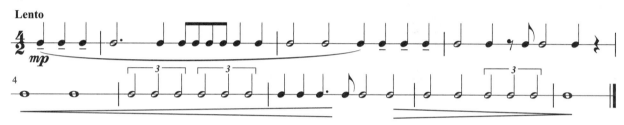

373

Waltz

374

Andante

Duets

375

Allegro

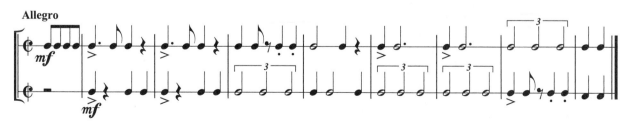

376

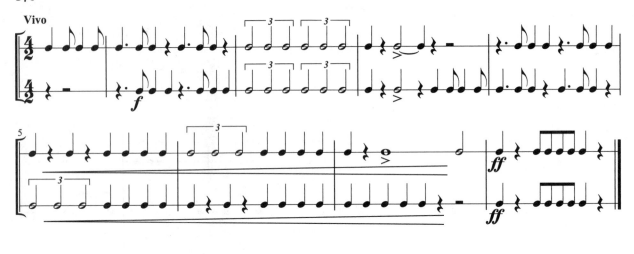

377

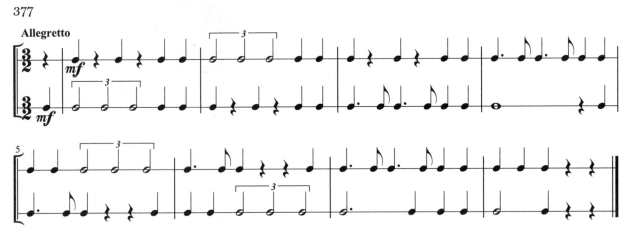

D. Compound (Super) Duplets (Chapter 18)

The following rhythms include **compound duplets**, also called **super duplets**: two notes that occur in the space of three beats. To prepare, conduct rhythm 378 in three. In mm. 3–4, perform only the notes with stems up, while imagining the duplet division (stems down).

378

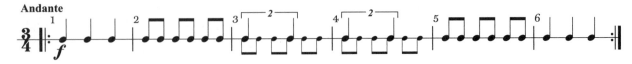

Simple meter

Rhythm 379 is a *palindrome*; mm. 5–8 are the exact reverse (retrograde) of mm. 1–4. In mm. 3 and 6, imagine the duplet division, but articulate only the first note of the measure and the second note of the second duplet.

Duets

386

387

388

Compound meter

Conduct rhythms 389a and 389b in two, keeping the same tempo for each. Practice until the compound (super) duplets are evenly spaced.

389a

Andante ($\quad$ = 76)

389b

Andante ($\quad$ = 76)

398

399

400

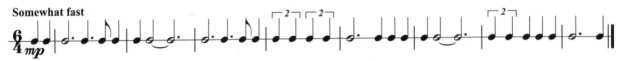

401

402

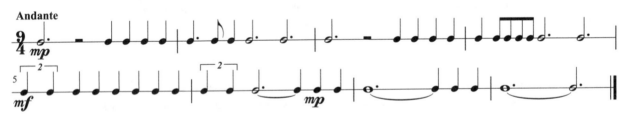

Duets and Trio

403

404

405

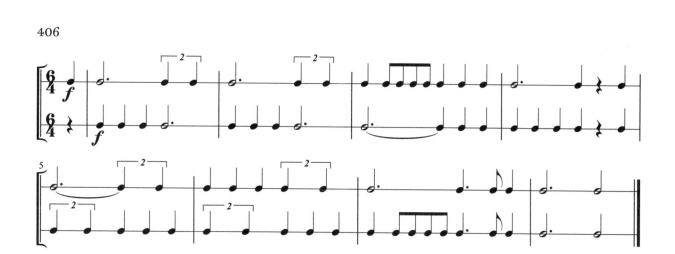

406

E. Hemiola (Chapter 19)

Six equal note values may be divided into two groups of three or three groups of two. When one of these divisions is prevalent, a temporary change to the other creates *hemiola*. Perhaps the most common example of hemiola occurs when two dotted-half notes are replaced by three half notes (examples 1 and 2), but any values in the ration 3:2 also create hemiola.

First, tap both parts, then perform one part while tapping the other.

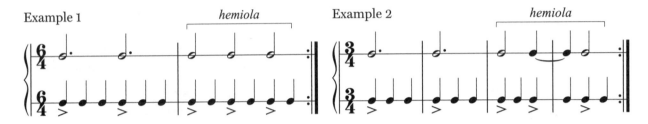

As in example 2, hemiola may occur over two measures.

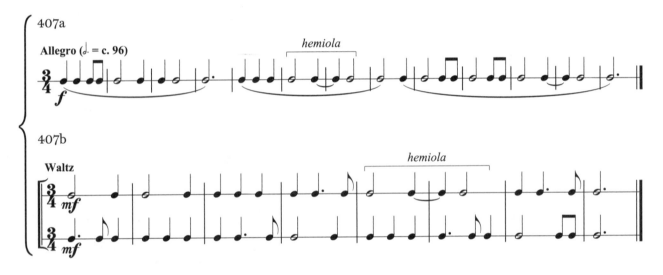

Conduct rhythms 408a and 408b as the meter signature indicates (in two for $\frac{6}{8}$ and in three for $\frac{3}{4}$), but switch your conducting in mm. 3–4 and 7–8.

Compound meter

409

413

414

Allegro

5

Simple meter

415

Adagio

5

416

Cheerfully

Duets

417

Lento

F. Combined Beat Divisions (3:2 and 2:3) in Simple Meters (Chapter 20)

Practice rhythms 419a and 419b by tapping the upward stems with your right hand and the downward stems with your left. Count each exercise with one beat per bar.

423

424

425

426

427

428

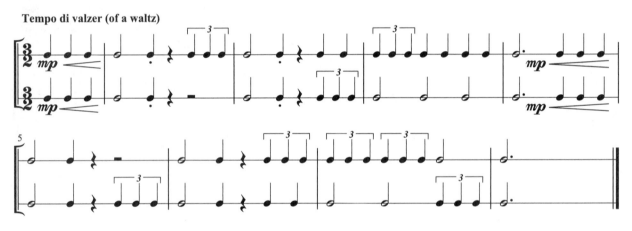

429

G. Combined Beat Divisions (3:2 and 2:3) in Compound Meters (Chapter 21)

430

436

437

Chromatic Harmony and Form

Sight-Singing

A. Tonicizations, Modulations, and Small Forms (Chapters 22–23)

Changing meter and tonicizations

645   Johannes Brahms, *Variations on a Hungarian Song*, Op. 21, No. 2

646   Jim Webb, "Galveston"

Gal-ves-ton,   oh,   Gal-ves - ton,   I still hear your sea winds blow-ing,

647   Gustav Mahler, Symphony No. 2, fifth movement (adapted)

648   Piotr Ilyich Tchaikovsky, String Quartet in F Major, Op. 22, Scherzo (adapted)

649 "Love Grows Under a Wide Oak Tree" (traditional)

Love grows un-der a wide oak tree. Su-gar flows like can - dy.

Top of the moun-tain shines like gold when you kiss your lit-tle hon-ey sort-a

Fine — Dreams, dreams, sweet dreams, un-der the wide oak tree,____

dreams, dreams, sweet dreams, one for you and me! Oh,

650 Felix Mendelssohn, "Jagdlied" ("Hunting Song"), Op. 84, No. 3

651 Brahms, String Quartet No. 3 in B♭ Major, second movement

652 Mendelssohn, "Der Mond" ("The Moon"), Op. 86, No. 5

653 Mendelssohn, "Nachtlied" ("Night Song"), Op. 71, No. 6

654 Edvard Grieg, String Quartet in G Minor, Op. 27, third movement (adapted)

Ensemble Melodies

655 Ludwig van Beethoven, Piano Sonata in A♭ Major, Op. 110, first movement (adapted)

656 Beethoven, Gloria, from *Mass in C*, Op. 86

657 Elizabeth Jacquet de la Guerre, *Suite in D Minor*, second Rigaudon (adapted)

658 Wolfgang Amadeus Mozart, Clarinet Quintet, K. 581, fourth movement (adapted)

Modulations to V, III, and V

The next five melodies include modulation to V.

659   Mendelssohn, "Das erste Veilchen" ("The First Violets"), Op. 19, No. 2

660   Johann Sebastian Bach, No. 13 from *St. John Passion* (adapted)

661   Mozart, String Quartet in B♭ Major, K. 458, Menuetto (adapted)

662 Brahms, String Sextet No. 1 in B♭ Major, Rondo

663 Bach, *Cello Suite No. 1* in G Major, Courante

The next four melodies feature modulations to III.

664 George Frideric Handel, *Suite in D Minor*, Gigue

665 Fanny Mendelssohn Hensel, "Schöne Fremde" ("Beautiful Stranger")

666 Handel, *Suite in F♯ Minor* (G. 207), Gigue (adapted)

667 Henry Purcell, "Or if more influencing is to be brisk," from *From Rosy Bow'rs*

Recall that in minor keys, the key of the dominant is minor. The next five melodies include modulation to v.

668 Mendelssohn, "Erntelied" ("Harvest Song"), Op. 8, No. 4

669 Hensel, "Schwanenlied" ("Swan Song"), from *Six Songs*, Op. 1, No. 1

670   Mendelssohn, String Quartet in E♭ Major, Op. 12, fourth movement

671   Mendelssohn, "Suleika," Op. 34, No. 4 (adapted)

672   Mendelssohn, "Pagenlied" ("The Page's Song") (adapted)

Ensemble Melodies

The initial ensemble melodies emphasize modulations from I to V, i to III, and i to v.
Modulations to other keys are featured in the rest.

673 Mozart, *Allegro*

674 Joseph Haydn, String Quartet in C Major, Op. 20, No. 2, first movement (adapted)

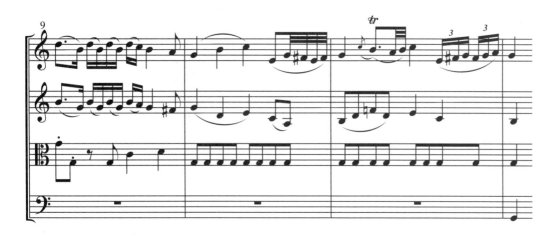

675 Bach, "Brunnquell aller Güter" ("Fountain of All Good Things")

676 Daniel Gottlob Turk, "Evening Song"

677 Bach, "Et in Spiritum Sanctum Dominum" ("And in the Holy Spirit"), from *Mass in B Minor*

678 Hensel, "Schilflied" ("Reed Song")

679   Beethoven, Piano Sonata in F Minor, Op. 2, No. 1, third movement (adapted)

680   Purcell, "A Farewell" (adapted)

B. More Contrapuntal Music, Modal Mixture, and the N⁶ and A⁶ Chords (Chapters 24–26)

Modulations to multiple keys

Ensemble Melodies

682 Johann Sebastian Bach, "Auf, auf! die rechte Zeit ist hier" ("Up, Up! The Right Time Is Here!")

683 Bach, "Jesu, deine Liebeswunden" ("Jesus, Your Dear Wounds")

684 Bach, "Dir, dir, Jehovah, will ich singen" ("To You, Jehovah, Will I Sing")

685 Henry Purcell, "Me Judah's daughters once caress'd," from *Harmonia Sacra*, vol. II (adapted)

686 George Frideric Handel, *Suite in B♭* (G. 33), Gigue

When a part exceeds your range, change octaves as inconspicuously as possible.

687 Bach, *Violin Partita No. 1* in B Minor, Courante

Play the accompaniment on the grand staff while singing the guide-tone melody in the top staff. Then accompany yourself while singing Bach's melody very slowly. Have the class sing the accompaniment and guide tones while someone performs Bach's melody.

Modal mixture

688   Johannes Brahms, String Sextet No. 2 in G Major, first movement (adapted)

689   Dan Fogelberg, "Longer"

Long-er than there've been fish-es in the o-cean, high-er than an-y bird ev-er flew,

Long-er than there've been stars up in the hea-vens, I've been in love with you.

690   Elton John and Bernie Taupin, "Your Song"

If I were a sculp-tor but then a-gain no, or a

man who makes po - tions in a trav-el - in' show, I

know it's not much but it's the do,

my gift is my song and this one's for you.

691   Gustav Mahler, "In diesem Wetter" ("In This Weather"), from *Kindertotenlieder*
(*Songs on the Death of Children*)

692 Ludwig van Beethoven, Piano Sonata in C Major, Op. 53 (*Waldstein*), first movement (adapted)

693 Brahms, *Liebeslieder Waltzer*, Op. 52, No. 3 (adapted)

694 Brahms, *Intermezzo* in E♭ Major, Op. 117, No. 1

695 Brahms, Piano Sonata No. 1 in C Major, first movement (adapted)

696 Beethoven, Symphony No. 4 in B♭ Major, Menuetto (adapted)

697 Felix Mendelssohn, "Neue Liebe" ("New Love"), Op. 19, No. 4

698 Mahler, "Die zwei blauen Augen von meinem Schatz" ("The Two Blue Eyes of My Sweetheart"), from *Lieder eines fahrenden Gesellen* (*Songs of a Wayfarer*) (adapted)

699 Beethoven, "Lustig, traurig" ("Funny, Sad"), WoO 54 (adapted)

Ensemble Melodies

700 Brahms, *Liebeslieder Walzer*, Op. 65, No. 14 (adapted)

701 Fanny Mendelssohn Hensel, "Lust'ge Vögel" ("Happy Birds")

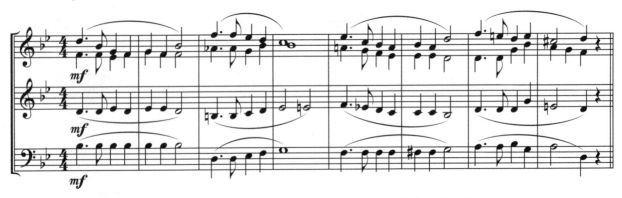

Some chromatic chords are easier to sing in context, so ensemble melodies that feature Neapolitan sixth and augmented-sixth chords appear before single-line melodies that imply the use of these chords.

702 Bach, Kyrie, from *Mass in B Minor*

Ky - ri - e e - lei - - - son, e - le - i - son

703 Beethoven, String Quartet in G Major, Op. 18, No. 2, third movement (Trio)

704 Hugo Wolf, "Ein stündlein wohl vor Tag" ("Just Before the Dawn")

705 Franz Schubert, "Die Liebe hat gelogen" ("Love Has Proved False")

Die Lie - be hat ge - lo - gen, die Sor - ge la - stet schwer,

Translation: Love has proved false, sorrow weighs heavily.

706 Beethoven, Bagatelle No. 1 in G Minor, from *Eleven Bagatelles*, Op. 119 (adapted)

707 Hensel, "Schon kehren die Vögel" ("Even the Birds Return")

708 Wolfgang Amadeus Mozart, Piano Sonata in F Major, K. 280, second movement (adapted)

709 Bach, Recitativo, from Cantata No. 51, *Jauchzet Gott in allen Landen* (*Praise God in All Lands*), BWV 51 (adapted)

so kann ein ___ schlech-tes ___ Lob ihm ___ den - noch wohl ___ - ge -

- fal - len.

Translation: Yet feeble praise can still please Him.

710 Bach, Agnus Dei, from *Mass in B Minor*

711   Joseph Haydn, String Quartet in F Major, Op. 74, No. 2, first movement (adapted)

Study the accidentals to determine the local keys.

712   Bach, No. 8 from *Mass in B Minor*

713 Bach, *Suite No. 2* for Orchestra (BWV 1067), Badinerie (adapted)

714   Mozart, Piano Sonata in F Major, K. 332, first movement (adapted)

715   Bach, *Partita No. 3* in C Minor, Gigue (adapted)

716   Bach, Sonata IV, from *Six Trio Sonatas*, BWV 528a

Solo Melodies

717 Hector Berlioz, *Symphonie fantastique*, Op. 15, Funeral March

718 Mendelssohn, "Des Mädchens Klage" ("The Maiden's Lament")

719 Brahms, *Liebeslieder Walzer*, Op. 65, No. 9

720 Mahler, "Nun will die Sonn' so hell aufgeh'n" ("Now the Sun Will Rise as Brightly"), from *Kindertotenlieder* (adapted)

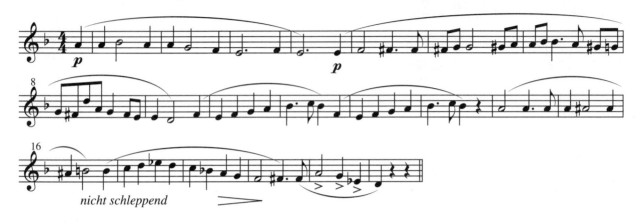

nicht schleppend

721 Jack Gold and John Barry, "Midnight Cowboy"

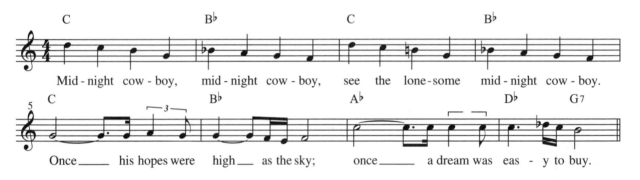

Mid-night cow-boy, mid-night cow-boy, see the lone-some mid-night cow-boy.

Once ____ his hopes were high ___ as the sky; once ____ a dream was eas - y to buy.

722 John Barry and Don Black, "Thunderball"

He always runs while o-thers walk, ____ he acts while o-ther men just talk, ____

723 Stephen Schwartz, "Turn Back, O Man"

Built while they dream, and in that dream-ing weep,

still will not hear _____ thine in-ner God pro - claim,

724   Schubert, "Der stürmische Morgen" ("The Stormy Morning"), from *Winterreise*

C. New Vocal Forms and More Chromatic Harmonies (Chapters 27–32)

As you sing the next sixteen melodies, harmonize them by realizing the chord symbols (when provided) or by employing the specified chromatic chords.

725   Joel Phillips, "Blues for Norton"

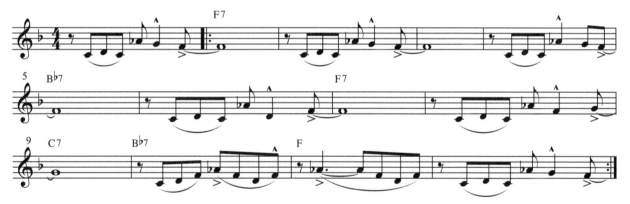

726 Hart A. Wand, "Dallas Blues"

727 Don Hecht and Alan W. Block, "Walkin' After Midnight"

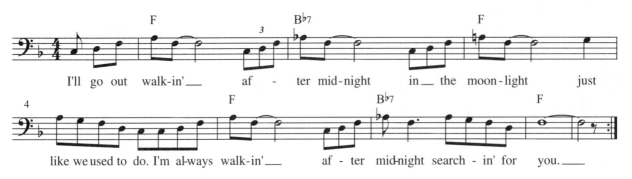

I'll go out walk-in'___ af - ter mid-night in__ the moon-light just

like we used to do. I'm al-ways walk-in'___ af - ter mid-night search - in' for you.___

728 W. C. Handy, "Memphis Blues"

729 J. Brandon Walsh, "The Broadway Blues" (adapted)

In the next three melodies, harmonize the chromatic neighbor tones with common-tone diminished seventh chords.

730 Frank Perkins and Mitchell Parish, "Stars Fell on Alabama"

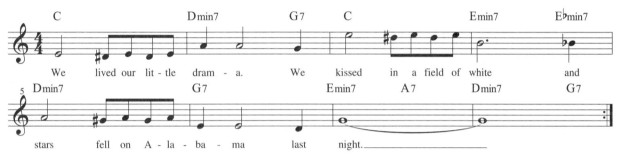

731 Richard Rodgers and Oscar Hammerstein II, "Sixteen Going on Seventeen," from *The Sound of Music*

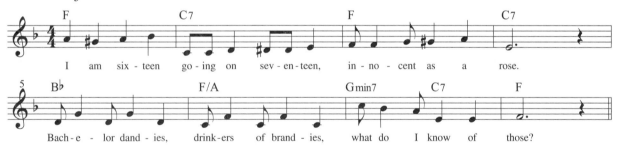

732 Robert Henning and Heinz Provost, "Intermezzo"

733   Paul Francis Webster and Dimitri Tiomkin, "The Green Leaves of Summer"
Variation: In m. 7, play an A.^{6}

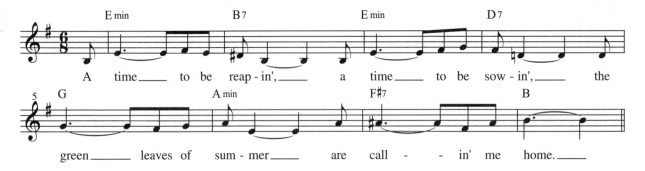

734   Fanny Mendelssohn Hensel, *Song No. 6* for piano
In mm. 4 and 8, harmonize the melody with A^6–V. In m. 6, use A^6–V in the key of IV.

735   Johann Strauss Jr., "The Beautiful Blue Danube" (adapted)
Conclude your harmonization with A^6–V in the key of vi.

In the next two melodies, employ the chromatic descending-fifth sequence.

736   Jerome Kern and Oscar Hammerstein II, "All the Things You Are"

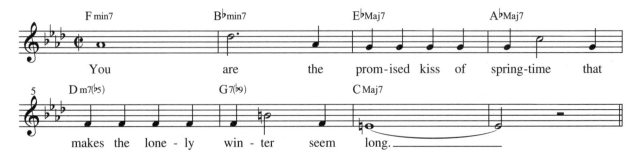

737   Jean Thielemans, "Bluesette"

738   "My Country, 'Tis of Thee" (traditional)

In m. 4, harmonize with a chromatic cadential $^6_4$ followed by a deceptive resolution. Try another variation: harmonize mm. 4–6 with I–V$^6_5$/vi–V$^6_5$/V–V$^{6-6}_{4-5}$–I.

739   Joe Burke, "Tiptoe Through the Tulips"

Harmonize the beginning with a chromatic 5–6 sequence. (Follow a half-note harmonic rhythm.) On beat 4 of m. 4, use a borrowed chord.

740   Johannes Brahms, String Sextet No. 2 in G Major, fourth movement

Harmonize mm. 6–7 with an ascending 5–6 sequence. (Begin with vi and employ a dotted-quarter-note harmonic rhythm.) Modulate to V.

D. Variations, Rondo, and Sonata Forms (Chapters 31–32)

For the next two melodies, one person performs the ground bass repeatedly while the other improvises melodic variations.

741   Henry Purcell, ground bass from "A New Ground," an arrangement of "Here the Deities Approve," from *Musick's Hand-Maid*

742 Purcell, ground bass from "Ground in Gamut," from *Musick's Hand-Maid*

743 Johann Sebastian Bach, Aria, from Cantata No. 51, *Jauchzet Gott in allen Landen* (*Praise God in All Lands*), BWV 51

Translation: Highest One, renew your goodness with every new morning.

Melodies 744–745 feature a theme followed by sectional variations. Compare the themes with that of melody 658.

744 Brahms, *Variations on an Original Theme* for piano, Op. 21, No. 1

(a) Theme

(b) Variation 1

(c) Variation 3

(d) Variation 4

745 Ludwig van Beethoven, *Variations for Piano*, Op. 76 (adapted)

(a) Theme

(b) Variation 1

(c) Variation 3

746 Joseph Haydn, Piano Trio No. 39 in G Major, third movement (adapted)

This melody is an example of rondo.

The remaining melodies are from sonata-form movements.

747 Beethoven, Piano Sonata in D Minor, Op. 31, No. 2 (*Tempest*), first movement (adapted)

748 Haydn, Piano Sonata No. 45 in E♭ Major, first movement (adapted)

749   Wolfgang Amadeus Mozart, Piano Sonata in A Minor, K. 310, first movement (adapted)

750   Mozart, Piano Concerto in C Major, K. 467, first movement (adapted)

751 Robert Schumann, String Quartet in A Minor, Op. 41, No. 1, fifth movement (adapted)

This final melody is an entire vocal composition, whose features recall many of the challenges you have worked hard to master.

752 Anton Bruckner, "Locus Iste"

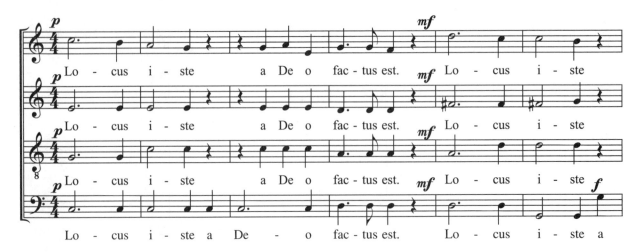

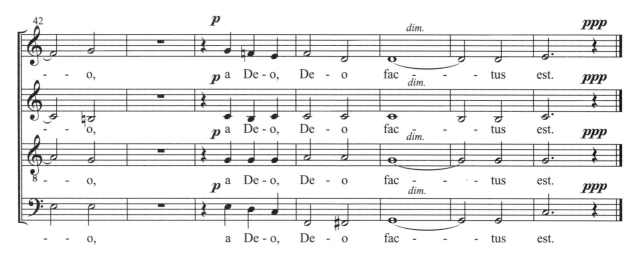

Translation: This place was made by God, a priceless sacrament, beyond reproach.

Rhythm-Reading

The rhythms in this part include performance instructions in English, Italian, German, and French. Each term is defined at its first appearance. Occasionally, phrasing slurs indicate a specific grouping. Where performance indications are not given, make your own choices regarding how to achieve the most musical performance.

The two-part and ensemble exercises can be performed with a partner, with one person performing each part; as an ensemble, with several persons performing each part; by tapping the lower part with the left hand, the upper part with the right; on the keyboard with two different notes; by singing one part while tapping/playing the other.

A. Changing Meters (Chapters 22–24)

Conduct the meter changes indicated, paying particular attention to how you show the dynamic changes with your conducting gestures.

438

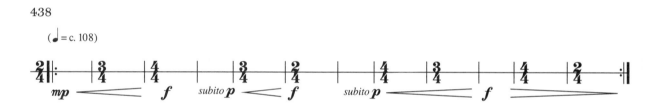

Note-value constant (note-value equivalence)

Sometimes changes of meter include an indication to show that the *note values* of the outgoing meter remain the same in the new one; for example, ♪=♪ or ♩=♩ or ♩.=♩. When no such indication is present, this note-value equivalence is assumed.

439

445

Etwas langsam (Somewhat slowly)

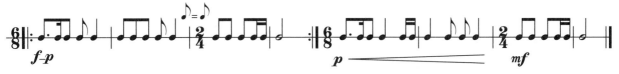

446

Leicht (Light)

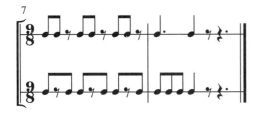

447

Animé

448

Schnell (Fast)

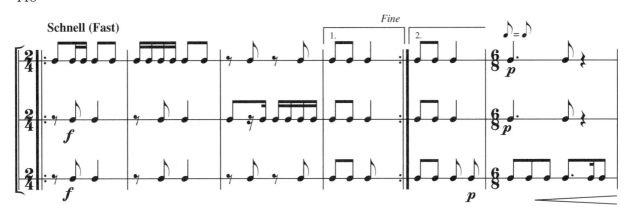

D.C. al Fine

Beat-unit constant (beat-unit equivalence)

For this type of meter change, two different note values are made equivalent in duration; for example, ♪=♪. or ♩=♩. Consequently, the duration of the beats will stay the same but the beat division will change.

Rhythms 449a and 449b sound identical. Conduct them in duple meter throughout while keeping the same duration for each beat.

459

Dual meter signatures

When meter changes recur, multiple meter signatures indicate the pattern of changes.

460

Tempo di Huapango

461

Allegro

462

Modéré

463

Allegretto

464

Ruhig (Peacefully)

465

Allegro

466   Joaquin Rodrigo, *Concierto de Aranjuez*, first movement (adapted)

Allegro con spirito

cresc. poco a poco

467

Moderato

468

B. Super-Subdivided Beats in Slow Tempos (Chapters 25–26)

In slow tempos, super-subdivided beats may be indicated with multiple beams. To maintain accurate counting, conduct the beat divisions.

- Conduct the normal beat pattern, but articulate each beat division with a "click" or "tick" in your gestures.
- Conduct the beat division as separate beats: in $\frac{2}{4}$, for example, conduct in four; in $\frac{6}{8}$, conduct in six.

Simple-duple meter

469

Langsam (Slow)

470

Lent

Simple-triple meter

Compound-duple meter

Conduct in six as indicated, or according to your teacher's instructions.

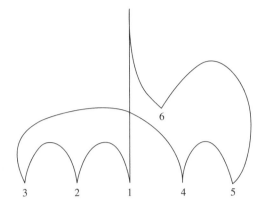

480

Adagio (♪ = 72)

$\frac{6}{8}$ *mf*

481

Einfach (Simply)

$\frac{6}{8}$ *mf*

482

Langsam

$\frac{6}{8}$ *pp*

483

Adagio

$\frac{6}{8}$ *mf*

484

C. More Syncopation: Ragtime and Jazz (Chapters 27–28)

Ragtime

Perform in *tempo giusto* (strict time), without swing or *rubato*.

485   Scott Joplin, "The Easy Winners"

Not fast

486

Andante

7

487

Not fast

7

488   Joplin, "Solace" (adapted)

Very slow march time

7

489   Joplin, "Bethena" (adapted)

Cantabile

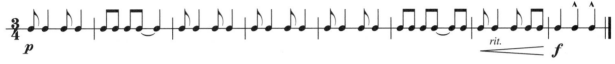

490   Joseph Lamb, "Bohemia" (adapted)

Moderately

8

491

Andante

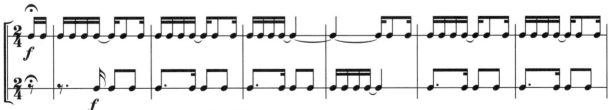

492   Joplin, "Solace" (adapted)

Very slow march time

7

Jazz

The next rhythms should be "swung," with a long-short division of the beat, similar to that of compound meter's ♩♪ rhythm. Where no swing is indicated, perform the rhythm as written.

STRATEGIES FOR SWUNG RHYTHMS

- Perform the rhythm in strict time, then "relax" the offbeats.
- Experiment by accenting the offbeats.
- Swing the rhythm from the start; set a tempo and conduct a few measures while imagining the written rhythm in its swung fashion.

493

494   Johnny Green, "Body and Soul" (adapted)

495   Billy Strayhorn, "Take the 'A' Train" (adapted)

496

497   Antonio Carlos Jobim, "One Note Samba" (adapted)

498 Phil Woods, "Waltz for a Lovely Wife" (adapted)

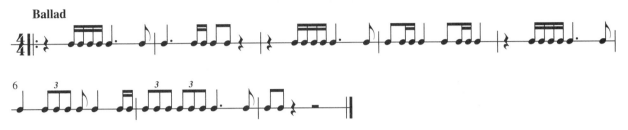

499 Thelonious Monk, " 'Round Midnight" (adapted)

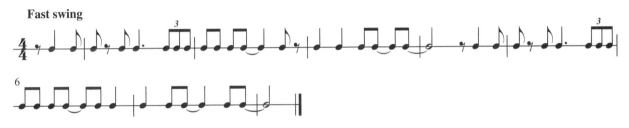

500

501

D. Asymmetric Meters (Chapters 29–30)

The beat divisions of aymmetric meters are unequal. Thus, meters of five or seven may sound like alternations between two or three different meters. Meters of five usually have two beats (dividing into 3+2 or 2+3). Meters of seven can have two beats (4+3 or 3+4) or three (3+2+2, 2+2+3, or 2+3+2). When a meter's lower number is 8, beams help to indicate the grouping; when the bottom number is 4, analyze the longest and shortest note values of each measure to reveal any grouping patterns.

Perform the following two preparatory exercises by conducting in two throughout, keeping the eighth note steady and constant.

- In mm. 3–4, change your conducting to a compound beat followed by a simple beat.
- Make sure that the beats in mm. 3–4 are *not* of the same duration; the second beat will feel "square" in comparison with the "round" feel of the first beat.
- Tap eighth notes with one hand while conducting the meter with the other.

Two beats per measure

503

Animé

504

Munter (Animated)

505

Lent

506

Modéré

507

Lustig

514

Moderato

Two or three beats per measure

515

Moderato

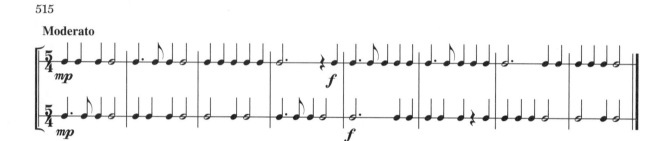

516

Nicht schnell (Not fast)

517

Animé

518

Allegro

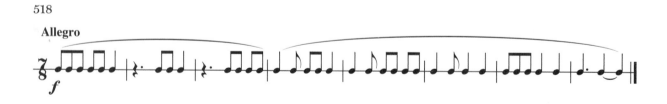

519

Modéré

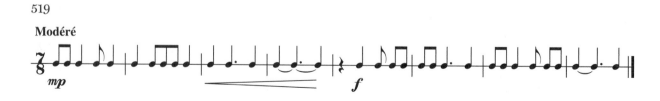

520

Assez vif (Very lively)

521

522

Calmly

523

Allegro (3+2+2)

524

Lebhaft

525

Slowly (2+3+2)

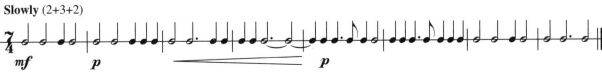

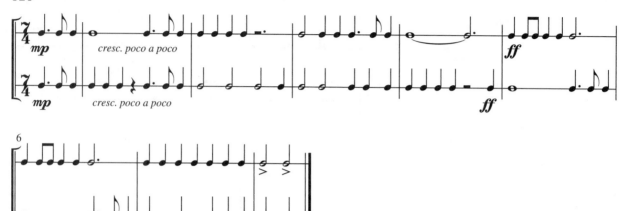

E. Combined Beat Divisions (3:4) (Chapters 31–32)

Rhythms 527a and 527b help you understand kinesthetically how these two beat divisions (four groups of three and three groups of four) relate to each other.

STRATEGIES

- Tap the lower part with your left hand, the upper part with your right.
- Sing aloud the rhythmic syllables of the lower and upper parts as instructed by your teacher.
- Practice the exercise until the 3:4 relationship is accurate and you can sing the rhythmic syllables of either part independently.

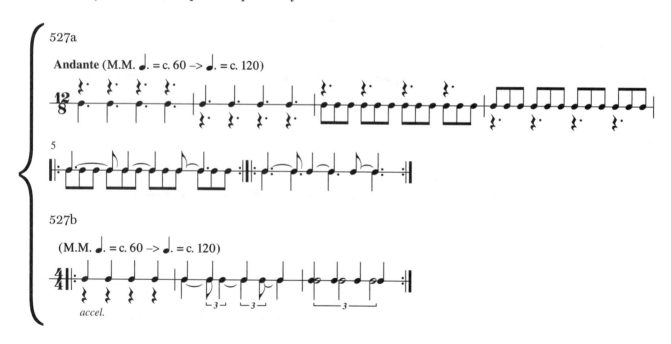

Simple meters

528

Andante

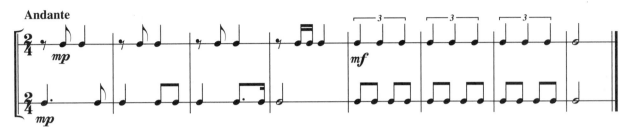

529

Allegretto

530

Allegro

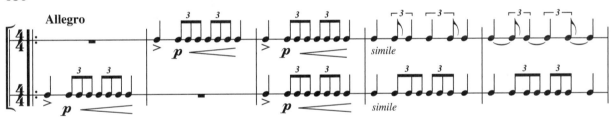

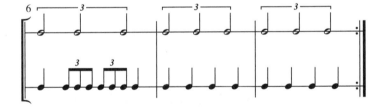

531

Gracieux

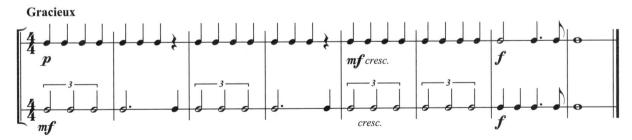

Part III Chromatic Harmony and Form

536

537

538

539

Compound meters

540

543

544

545

546

547

548

549

Part III Chromatic Harmony and Form

PART IV

The Twentieth Century and Beyond

A. Modal and Pentatonic Melodies Revisited (Chapter 33)

Because composers renewed their interest in modes and pentatonic scales during the last century, we revisit them here. First, please review all the modal and pentatonic melodies from Part I.

753   Joel Phillips, "Windsong," from *Pieces for Children*

754   Ernest Chausson, "La Cigale," from *Four Songs*, Op. 13, No. 4

755   Claude Debussy, "Bruyères," from *Préludes*, Book II

756 Debussy, "Général Lavine," from *Préludes,* Book II

757 Germaine Tailleferre, Sonata in C♯ Minor for Violin and Piano

758 Rebecca Clarke, Sonata for Viola and Piano, first movement
Add a second performer in m. 8, when a second line enters.

759 Maurice Ravel, "Là-bas, vers l'église" ("Near the Church")

760 Phillips, "Reflections," from *Pieces for Children* (adapted)

B. Precursors to Atonal Music: Collections and Sets (Chapters 34–35)

Late nineteenth- and early twentieth-century music included extended ranges and techniques for instruments; complex rhythms and meters; and chromaticism so extensive that aural retention of a tonal center was difficult. The initial melodies demonstrate some of these challenges.

761 Piotr Ilyich Tchaikovsky, Symphony No. 4, first movement (adapted)

762 Hugo Wolf, "Ein Stündlein wohl vor Tag" ("Just Before Daybreak")

763 Richard Strauss, from *Don Juan* (viola part)

764 Wolf, "In der Frühe" ("At Dawn")

innig und zart

pp *allmächlich verklingend*

765 Anton Webern, "Am Ufer" ("On the Shore"), from *Five Songs After Poems by Richard Dehmel*

766 Webern, "Helle Nacht" (Bright Night"), from *Five Songs After Poems by Richard Dehmel*

767 Alban Berg, "Liebesode" ("Ode of Love"), from *Seven Early Songs*

Singing with integer notation

Highly chromatic or atonal melodies may be sung with integers, with enharmonic pitches receiving the same integer name. In order to maintain accurate rhythms, abbreviate any multisyllable integer as shown.

768

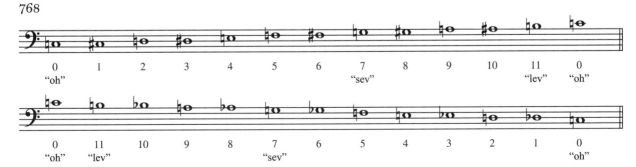

Look for familiar patterns, such as scales and tetrachords, to help orient your ear to unfamiliar music.

769   Béla Bartók, No. 10 from *44 Duets*, vol. I

Though the melodic pitches occur in the A harmonic minor scale, *ti* (7̂) resolves atypically.

770   Bartók, No. 7 from *44 Duets*, vol. I

Pitches 1–5 occur in the A harmonic minor scale, but here the centric pitch is D. Perform the pentachords to orient your ear to Bartók's melody, then perform the melody.

771   Igor Stravinsky, "Danse infernale de tous les sujets de Kastchéi" ("Infernal Dance of King Kastchéi's Subjects"), from *L'oiseau de feu (The Firebird)* (adapted)

Enharmonically, all the pitches belong to the E harmonic minor scale, but here B is the centric pitch. Sing this B-to-B scale to orient your ear to Stravinsky's scale, then sing his melody.

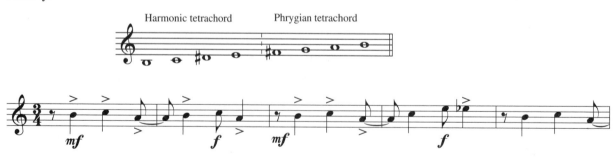

772   Bartók, No. 44 from *44 Duets*, vol. II (adapted)

Practice the familiar tetrachord patterns below to help tune Bartók's melody when you sing it.

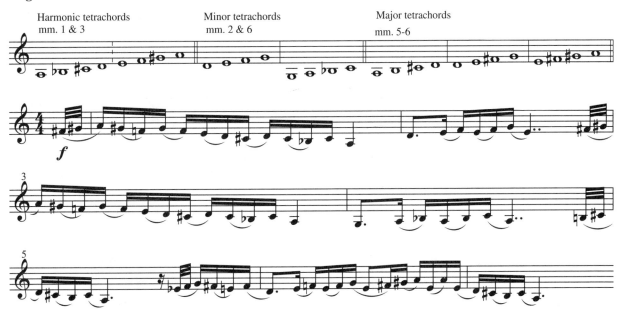

773   Joel Phillips, "Wallowtumble," from *Pieces for Children* (adapted)

Though the pitches in mm. 1–6 belong to a G melodic minor scale, the centric pitch is C.
This collection is called the Lydian-Mixolydian mode, or overtone scale.

Whole-tone études and melodies

779

780 Claude Debussy, "Les ingénues" ("Innocent Young Girls"), from *Fêtes galantes*, Book 2

781 Charles Ives, "September"

782 Phillips, "Two Lazy Cats," from *Pieces for Children*

Octatonic études and melodies

783

784

788 Alexander Scriabin, *Prelude*, Op. 74, No. 3

789 Andrew Carter, *Nunc dimittis (Now Let Your Servant Depart)*

Trichord études

The twelve trichords. Pitches 1–3 in each trichord are the prime form; pitches 4–6 are an inverted form.

Inverted forms of the twelve trichords.

In addition to identifying scales and modes in the next group of melodies, practice identifying trichords. Hints are provided in the first of these melodies.

816 Ives, "Premonitions"

Overlapping versions of the [016] trichord.

817 Bartók, No. 28 from *44 Duets*, vol. II

Trichord [024] begins and [016] ends each six-note melodic motive.

818 Bartók, *Two Rumanian Dances*, Op. 8a, No. 1 (adapted)

Look for the following trichords and scales: M. 1 (beat 4): [015] trichord. M. 6a: [014] trichord. Mm. 8–9: octatonic scale. M. 10: Lydian-Mixolydian mode (overtone scale). Mm. 10–end: [025], [026], and [027] trichords.

819   Paul Hindemith, *Concert Music for Strings and Brass,* Op. 50

Listen for subsets of the octatonic scale.

820   Arnold Schoenberg, *Das Buch der hängenden Gärten (The Book of the Hanging Gardens),* No. XIV

M. 1: [016] trichord outline ([0167] subsets). M. 1 (last eighth) to m. 3 (downbeat), and m. 10: whole-tone segments. Mm. 4–5: chromatic trichords. Mm. 7 and 9: "split-third triads" [0347].

821   Berg, Piano Sonata, Op. 1 (adapted)

Pickup and m. 5: [016]. Mm. 1, 3, 6, and downbeat of m. 7: [048]. M. 7 (beat 3) to m. 9 (beat 1): both forms of [014].

822   Webern, "Im Morgentaun" ("In the Morning Dew"), from *Five Songs from "Der siebente Ring" (The Seventh Ring) of Stefan George*

823   Berg, "Marie's Lullaby," from *Wozzeck*

824   George Crumb, "Dark Mother Always Gliding Near with Soft Feet"

825   Debussy, "C'est l'extase" ("Ecstasy"), from *Ariettes oubliées (Forgotten Little Arias)*

826 Webern, "Himmelfahrt" ("Heavenly Journey"), from *Five Songs After Poems by*
Richard Dehmel

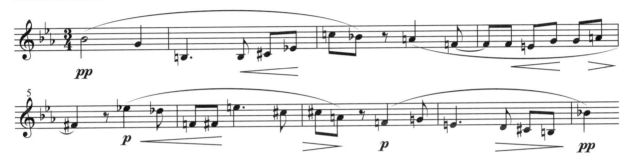

827 Webern, "Nächtliche Scheu" ("Nocturnal Fear"), from *Five Songs After Poems by*
Richard Dehmel

828 Webern, "Dies ist ein Lied für dich allein" ("This Is a Song for You Alone"), from
Five Songs from "Der siebente Ring" of Stefan George

829 Webern, "Im Windesweben war meine Frage" ("Weaving in the Wind Was My Question"), from *Five Songs from "Der siebente Ring" of Stefan George*

C. Ordered Collections and Twelve-Tone Music (Chapters 36–37)

830 Luigi Dallapiccola, "Liriche di Antonio Machado"
Note how the row consists of hexachords comprised of subsets of octatonic scales.

831 Morton Gould, *Jekyll and Hyde Variations for Orchestra*

If the excerpt were to continue, which pitch class would occur next?

832 Alban Berg, *Lyric Suite*, first movement (adapted)

833 Arnold Schoenberg, "Unentrinnbar" ("Inescapable"), from *Four Pieces for Mixed Chorus*, Op. 27, No. 1

834 Igor Stravinsky, Four Trios from *Agon*

Perform the pitches forward and backward to discover how the composer organized his twelve-tone fugue subject.

835 Schoenberg, *De profundis* (*Out of the Depths*), Op. 50B.

Translation: "Out of the depths I call to You, God."

836   Berg, Violin Concerto, first movement

The row, P_7, is the first twelve pcs. Mm. 10ff. are I_7. Consider pcs 1–4 and 5–8 to be ordered segments: the second is T_2 of the first. Consider pcs 9–12 to be another ordered segment: the whole-tone tetrachord, 4-21 [0246].

837   Schoenberg, *Variations for Orchestra*, Op. 31

838   Webern, "In der Fremde" ("In a Foreign Land"), from *Four Songs for Soprano and Orchestra*, Op. 13

This melody may sound similar to that of Webern's twelve-tone melodies, but it is not twelve-tone. This technique was a natural outgrowth of the atonal musical language composers were already developing in their music.

D. More Rhythmic Challenges (Chapters 38–40)

The remaining melodies feature rhythmic variety typical of music of the last hundred years. They also manipulate pitches in all the various ways you have studied so far—from the use of modes to sets and rows.

840   Igor Stravinsky, "Royal March," from *L'histoire du soldat* (*The Soldier's Tale*) (adapted)

Lydian mode

841 Stravinsky, Theme and Variations, from *Octet for Wind Instruments* (adapted)

Octatonic scale

842 Béla Bartók, No. 29 from *44 Duets*, vol. II

This melody moves from Dorian to Mixolydian.

843 Joel Phillips, "Holiday Round 2009" (round in 3 parts)

This melody is also Dorian.

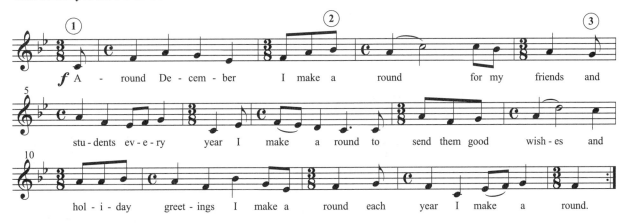

A - round De - cem - ber I make a round for my friends and stu - dents ev - e - ry year I make a round to send them good wish - es and hol - i - day greet - ings I make a round each year I make a round.

844 Bartók, No. 30 from *44 Duets*, vol. II

845 Deborah Koenigsberg, String Quartet, third movement (adapted)

846 Rebecca Oswald, *Finding the Murray River*

847 Phillips, "Gambolroister," from *Pieces for Children* (adapted)

This free use of all diatonic pitches is called pandiatonicism.

This melody is based on the minor pentatonic scale.

849   Bartók, No. 19 from *44 Duets*, vol. I

850

851   Olivier Messiaen, "Danse de la fureur, pour les sept trompettes" ("Dance of Frenzy, for the Seven Trumpets"), from *Quartet for the End of Time*

Mm. 1–4 are predominantly whole tone, and mm. 5–6 are octatonic.

Translation: We praise You, we bless You, we worship You.

853 Leonard Bernstein, *Kaddish* (Symphony No. 3) (adapted)

This work features a twelve-tone ground bass set to an asymmetrical meter.

854 Luigi Dallapiccola, *Quaderno musicale di Annalibera* (*Musical Notebook of Annalibera*), No. 4

Treat this melody as a duet or as a play-and-sing solo.

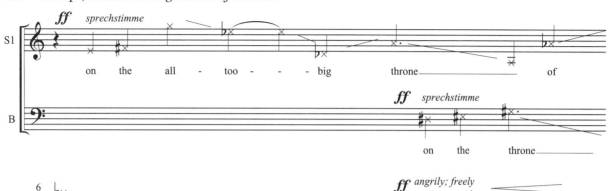

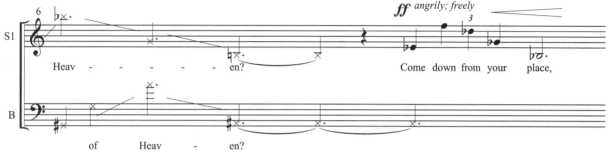

856 Anton Webern, "Ave Regina Coelorum" ("Hail, Queen of Heaven"), Op. 18, No. 3

There are three row forms: P_4, I_4, and RI_4. The last pc of I_4 (G♯, in m. 7) is also the first pc of RI_4.

Rhythm-Reading

A. Quintuplets and Septuplets

The first two preparatory exercises present divisions and subdivisions of the beat in a graduated manner. Conduct the rhythms in duple meter throughout while keeping the same duration for each beat. Aim for equally divided tuplets.

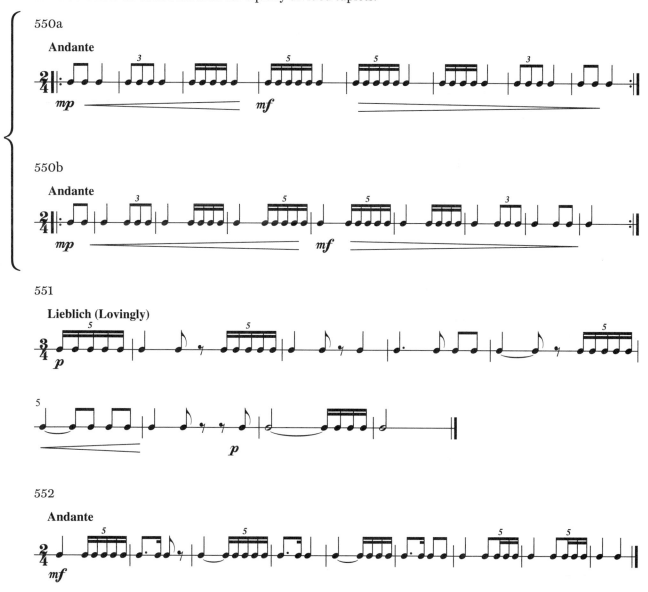

550a

Andante

550b

Andante

551

Lieblich (Lovingly)

552

Andante

553

Stark (Strong)

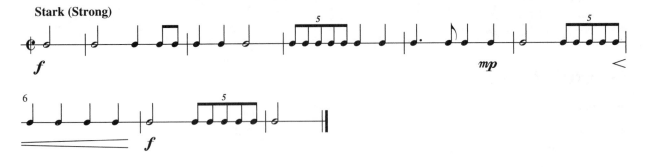

554

Sustained

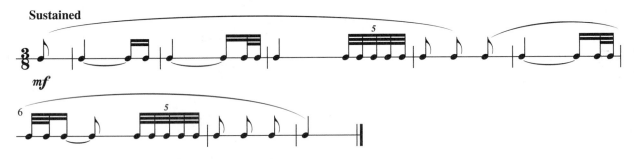

555

Andante

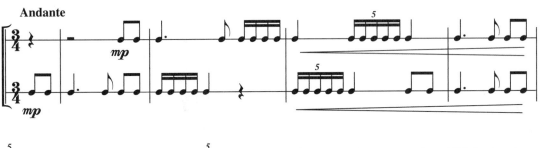

560

Conduct the next two preparatory rhythms in duple meter throughout while keeping the same duration for each beat. Aim for equally divided tuplets.

561a

561b

566

567

568

569

Joyeux (Joyfully)

570

Ruhig

571

$\quad \bullet \cdot = 60$

B. More Asymmetric Meters

Quintuple meters at slow tempos

Practice the conducting patterns below for use in slow-tempo quintuple meters. Make sure your conducting gestures convey any dynamic changes in the rhythms.

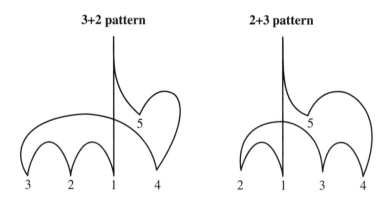

3+2 pattern　　　　**2+3 pattern**

572

Slowly

573

Lent

574

575

Ruhig

576

Calmly

577

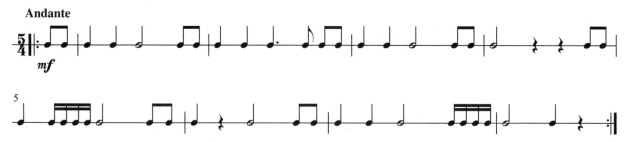

Septuple meters at slow tempos

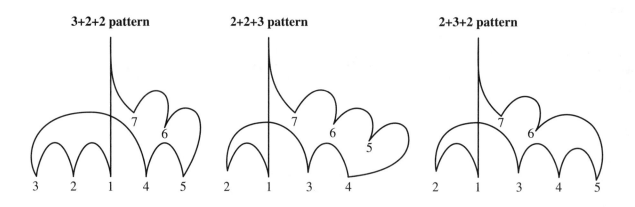

3+2+2 pattern

2+2+3 pattern

2+3+2 pattern

Practice the conducting patterns below for use in slow-tempo quintuple meters. Notice how each pattern represents a modified triple-meter conducting pattern.

578

583

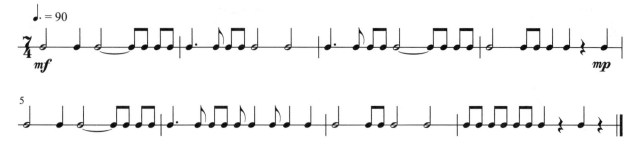

584

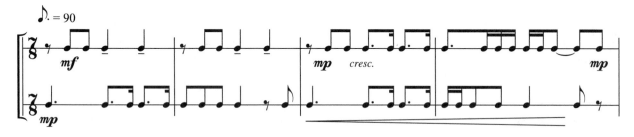

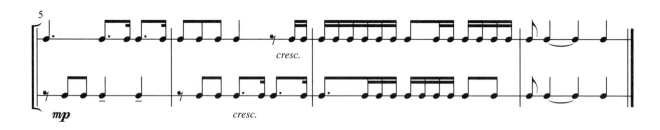

The following rhythms involve changes between asymmetric and symmetric meters.

585

Assez vite

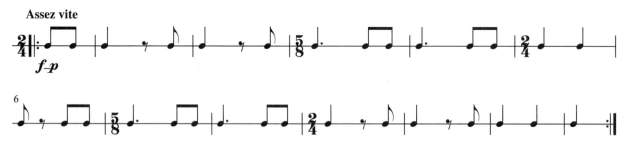

586

590

591

592

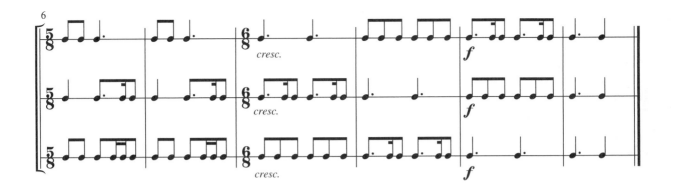

C. Characteristic Dance Rhythms

593

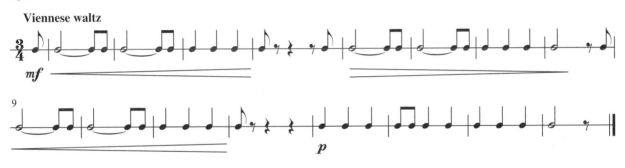

594

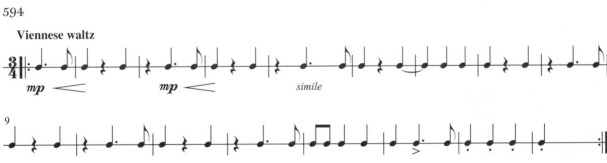

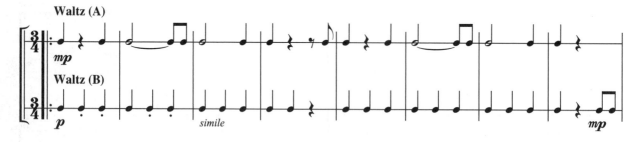

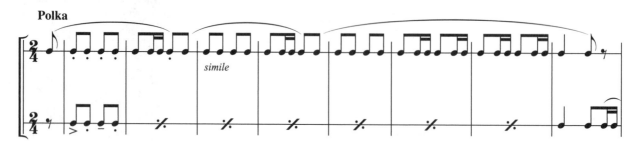

599

Mazurka ($\quad$ = 112)

600

Mazurka ($\quad$ = 60)

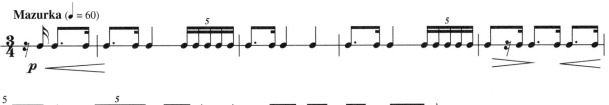

601

Tango ($\quad$ = 60)

602

603

604

Part IV The Twentieth Century and Beyond

605

606

607

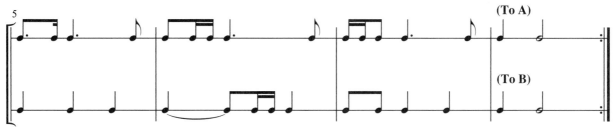

608

D. Rhythms of the Spoken Word

611   William Shakespeare, from Sonnet XLIII

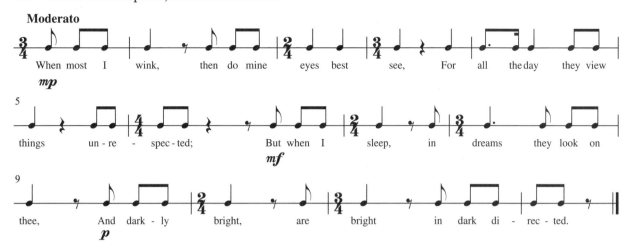

612   Robert Frost, from "Dust of Snow"

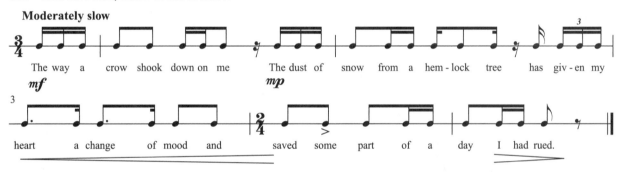

613   Alexander Pope, from "Ode on Solitude"

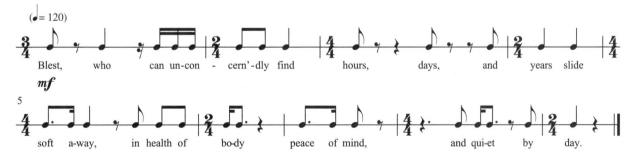

614 Emily Dickinson, from "A Narrow Fellow in the Grass"

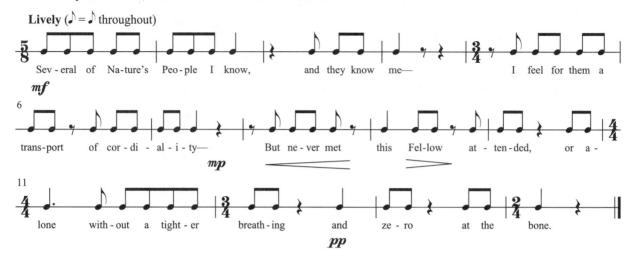

615 William Ernest Henley, from "Rondel"

616 Emily Dickinson, from "The Spider Holds a Silver Ball"

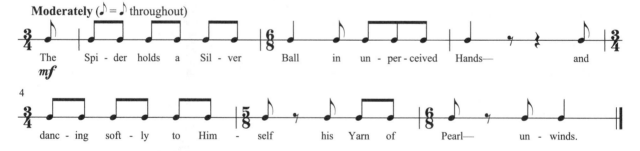

617   William Blake, "Ah Sunflower"

E. Tempo and Meter Modulation

Using common divisions and subdivisions

The first exercise presents tempo modulation that gradually slows. Notice the indicated tempo changes, and determine how these are calculated mathematically. Conduct the exercise in duple meter throughout. As indicated, keep the value of the beat division constant.

618

619

620

621

622

623

627

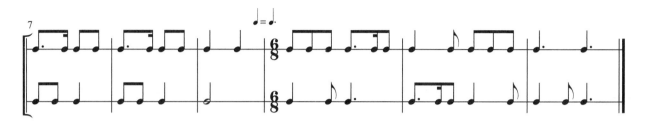

Using tuplets

628

629

630

631

632

633

F. Twentieth-Century Concepts and Literature

The following rhythms feature obscured meters and polymeters.

634

635

636

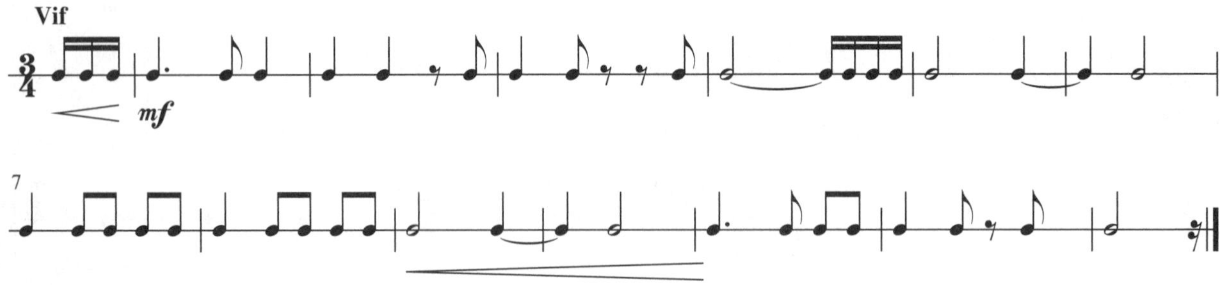

637

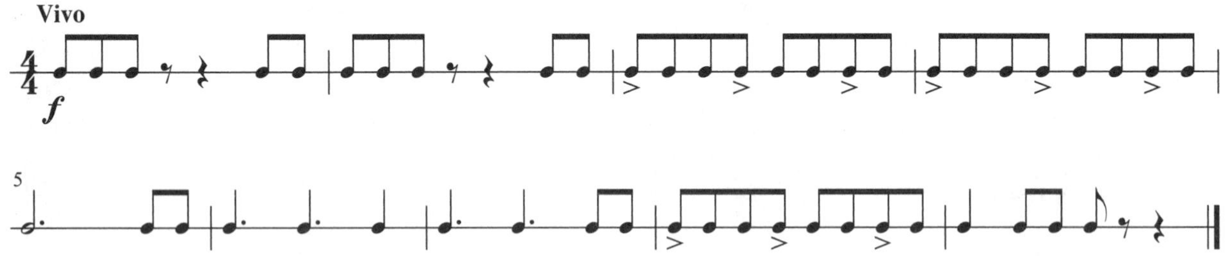

638

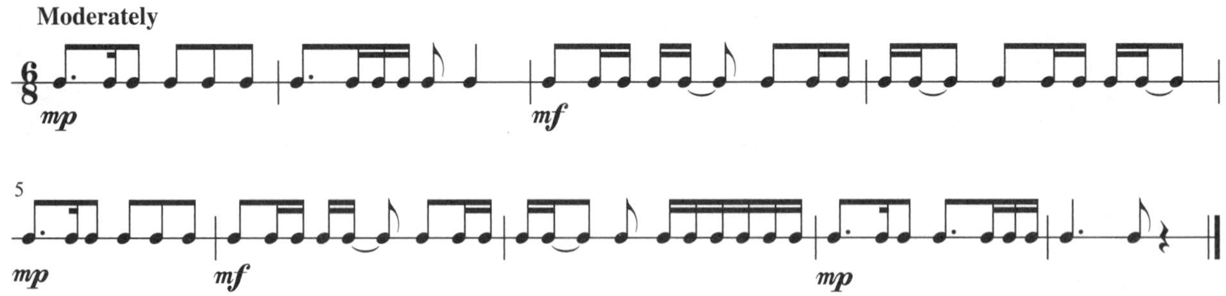

639

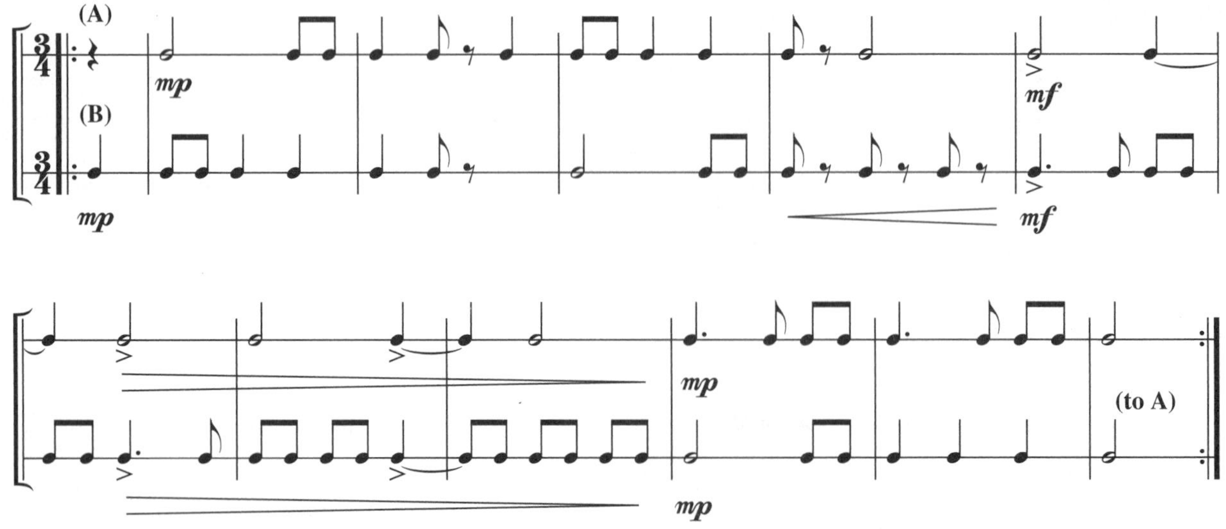

The following exercises include ametric rhythms, rhythms with added values, and non-retrogradable rhythms. Quietly tap the smallest note value as you sing the rhythm. Or quietly sing the smallest note value on a neutral syllable while you tap the rhythm.

642

643

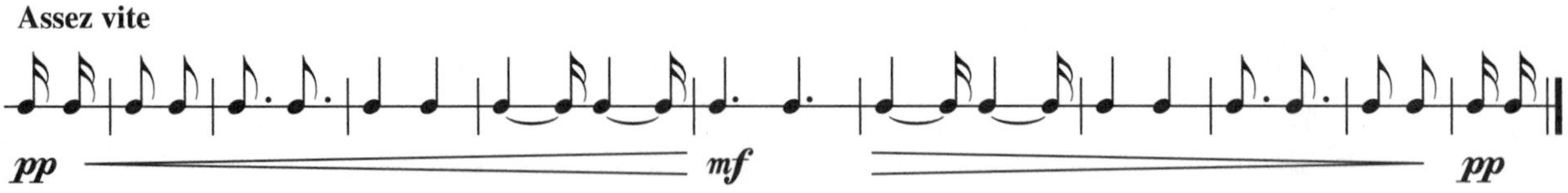

644

645

646

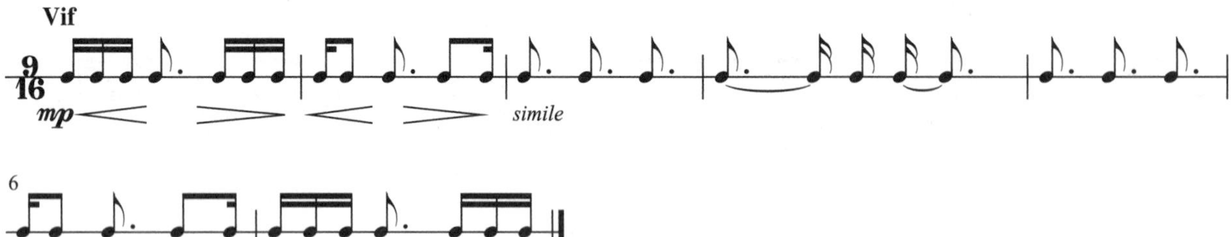

647

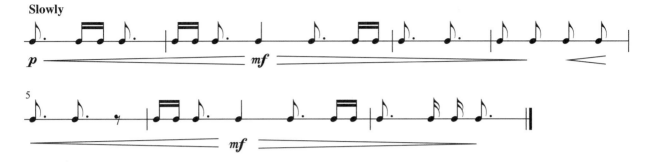

5

648

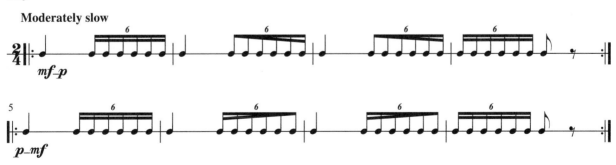

The next five exercises include "feathered beams," which indicate an increase or decrease in tempo within the beat. Conduct throughout, keeping strict time. Aim for clear accelerations and decelerations that do not lengthen or shorten the quarter-note beat.

649

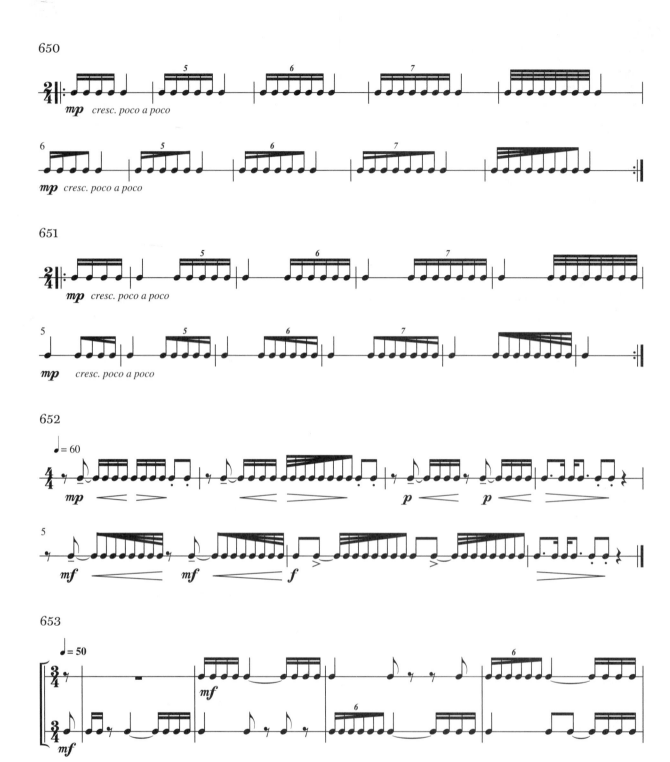

Isorhythm and serialized durations

654

From the Literature

657 Olivier Messiaen, "Danse de la fureur, pour les sept trompettes" ("Dance of Fury for the Seven Trumpets"), from *Quatour pour la fin du temps* (*Quartet for the End of Time*) (adapted)

658 Messiaen, "Danse de la fureur" (adapted)

659 Elliott Carter, *Eight Etudes and a Fantasy for Woodwind Quartet*, No. 9, Fantasy (adapted)

660 Luigi Dallapiccola, *Goethe-Lieder*, No. 2 (adapted)

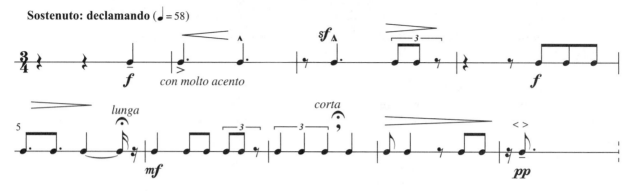

661 Claude Debussy, *Syrinx* (adapted)

662 Edgard Varèse, *Density 21.5* (adapted)

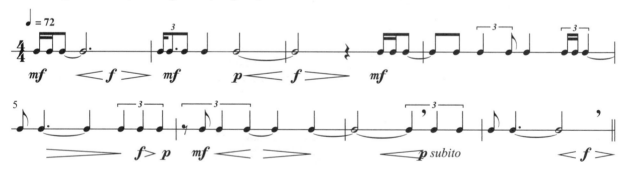

663   Charles Ives, Sonata for Violin and Piano, third movement, "The Revival" (adapted)

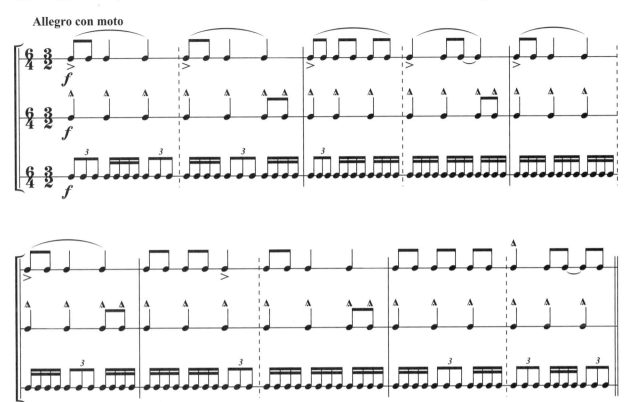

Improvisation

Throughout the book, many improvisation lessons may be performed repeatedly to reinforce each new concept you learn.

Lesson 1: Improvisation with Rhythmic Cells (Chapters 2ff.)

Improvise short rhythmic phrases based on these eight familiar beat patterns.

- Create phrases in simple-duple, -triple, or -quadruple meter.
- Feel free to substitute a rest for any note in any pattern.
- Sing the rhythms while conducting, with a counting system if your teacher requires it.
- Always sing dynamically, with inflection and accentuation to make your performance musical and interesting.
- Don't feel obliged to use every beat pattern in your phrases; you can often make musical, interesting phrases with only a few patterns.

Examples

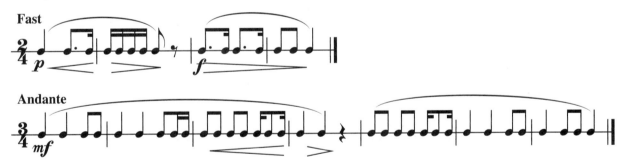

GROUP IMPROVISATION

- Your teacher will establish a tempo and meter that everyone will conduct together. A leader improvises a two-measure rhythm, which the class echoes by tapping, while continuing to conduct. Another leader improvises a new two-measure rhythm, again echoed by the class. Continue until everyone has been the leader. Leaders should use dynamics and accents to make their rhythms as musical as possible.
- As a variation, follow the same procedure but perform in duets, alternating between leader and follower.
- Improvise a rhythmic canon. The leader improvises a two-measure rhythmic pattern, which the follower then echoes, strictly in time. While the follower performs

the echo, the leader improvises a new pattern. Since the new patterns and the echoes overlap, both leader and follower must listen to their partner's part while performing their own.

Lesson 2: Major and Minor Triads

Use the four rhythms below as a basis for improvising melodies. Always conduct as you perform.

(1)

Moderato

(2)

Waltz

(3)

March

(4)

Sweetly

A. Choose a rhythm above, and improvise a melody with just *do*, *mi*, and *sol* (1̂–3̂–5̂).

Sample solution with rhythm (1)

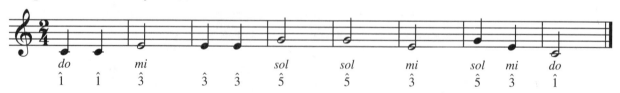

B. Choose a rhythm above, and improvise a melody with *do*, *me*, and *sol* (1̂–♭3̂–5̂).

Sample solution with rhythm (1)

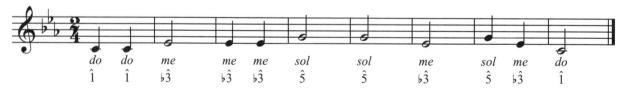

C. Duet: Choose a rhythm above, and work with a partner to perform exercises A and B again. Face each other and sing alternate measures.

D. Duet: Perform exercise C again, but this time begin each measure with the same pitch and syllable with which your partner ended the previous measure.

Sample solution with rhythm (3)

do mi sol sol sol sol mi mi sol mi mi sol sol sol sol mi mi sol do
$\hat{1}$ $\hat{3}$ $\hat{5}$ $\hat{5}$ $\hat{5}$ $\hat{5}$ $\hat{3}$ $\hat{3}$ $\hat{5}$ $\hat{3}$ $\hat{3}$ $\hat{5}$ $\hat{5}$ $\hat{5}$ $\hat{5}$ $\hat{3}$ $\hat{3}$ $\hat{5}$ $\hat{1}$

E. Duet: Now alternate each measure between *do, mi,* or *sol* ($\hat{1}$, $\hat{3}$, or $\hat{5}$) and *sol, ti,* or *re* ($\hat{5}$, $\hat{7}$, or $\hat{2}$).

Sample solution with rhythm (3)

do mi mi re re re ti do do mi re sol sol sol sol mi re sol sol
$\hat{1}$ $\hat{3}$ $\hat{3}$ $\hat{2}$ $\hat{2}$ $\hat{2}$ $\hat{7}$ $\hat{1}$ $\hat{1}$ $\hat{3}$ $\hat{2}$ $\hat{5}$ $\hat{5}$ $\hat{5}$ $\hat{5}$ $\hat{3}$ $\hat{2}$ $\hat{5}$ $\hat{5}$

Lesson 3: Major- and Minor-Key Melodies (Chapters 1–10)

A. Major-key melodies

Improvise short melodies from the embellished major pentachord. Play them and sing with solfège syllables or scale-degree numbers. Before starting, conduct in silence until you establish a comfortable, steady tempo. Always sing dynamically, with inflection and accentuation to make your performance musical and interesting.

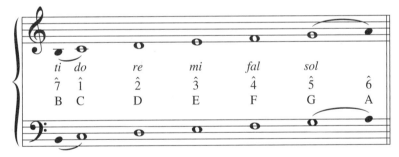

ti do re mi fal sol
$\hat{7}$ $\hat{1}$ $\hat{2}$ $\hat{3}$ $\hat{4}$ $\hat{5}$ $\hat{6}$
B C D E F G A

Example

Now organize the melodies into simple-duple, -triple, or -quadruple meter. At first, limit your rhythm to beat and beat division. As you improve, add beat subdivisions.

Example

B. Minor-key melodies

Combine the minor-key melodic segments below to create melodies in each of the following meters: simple duple, simple triple, simple quadruple; compound duple, compound triple, compound quadruple.

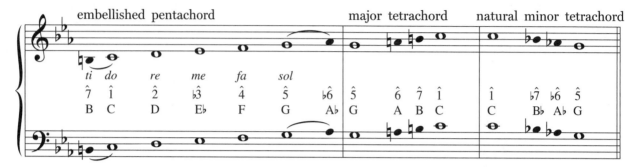

STRATEGIES

1. In melodic minor, complete the upper tetrachord. When *sol* rises to *la*, continue upward through *ti* to *do* ($\hat{5}$–$\hat{6}$–$\hat{7}$–$\hat{1}$). When *do* descends to *te*, continue downward through *le* to *sol* ($\hat{1}$–$\flat\hat{7}$–$\flat\hat{6}$–$\hat{5}$).

2. In harmonic minor, use the pitches of the embellished pentachord. Fall from *le* to *sol* ($\flat\hat{6}$–$\hat{5}$); rise from *ti* to *do* ($\hat{7}$–$\hat{1}$).

Examples

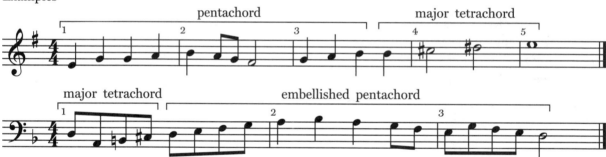

C. Major- and minor-key melodies

Now combine major- or minor-key melodic segments in simple and compound meters.

Example

Lesson 4: Major Pentatonic, Minor Pentatonic, and Modal Melodies (Chapters 5ff.)

Follow the procedures in Lesson 3 to improvise melodies in each scale and mode below.
Be sure to practice in both simple and compound meters.

Major pentatonic

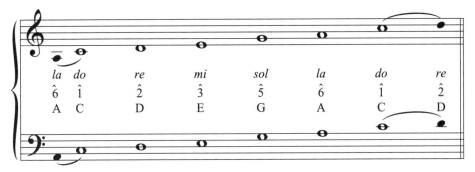

	la	*do*	*re*	*mi*	*sol*	*la*	*do*	*re*
	$\hat{6}$	$\hat{1}$	$\hat{2}$	$\hat{3}$	$\hat{5}$	$\hat{6}$	$\hat{1}$	$\hat{2}$
	A	C	D	E	G	A	C	D

Minor pentatonic

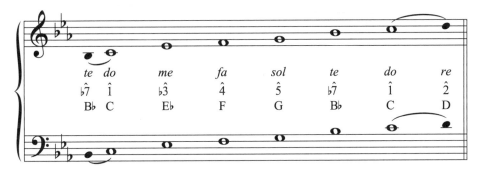

	te	*do*	*me*	*fa*	*sol*	*te*	*do*	*re*
	$\flat\hat{7}$	$\hat{1}$	$\flat\hat{3}$	$\hat{4}$	$\hat{5}$	$\flat\hat{7}$	$\hat{1}$	$\hat{2}$
	B♭	C	E♭	F	G	B♭	C	D

Dorian

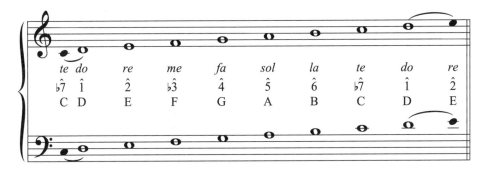

	te	*do*	*re*	*me*	*fa*	*sol*	*la*	*te*	*do*	*re*
	$\flat\hat{7}$	$\hat{1}$	$\hat{2}$	$\flat\hat{3}$	$\hat{4}$	$\hat{5}$	$\hat{6}$	$\flat\hat{7}$	$\hat{1}$	$\hat{2}$
	C	D	E	F	G	A	B	C	D	E

Aeolian

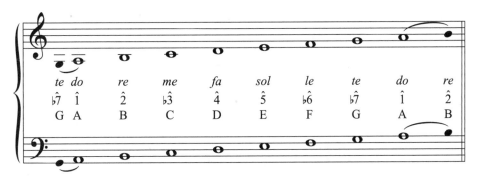

	te	*do*	*re*	*me*	*fa*	*sol*	*le*	*te*	*do*	*re*
	$\flat\hat{7}$	$\hat{1}$	$\hat{2}$	$\flat\hat{3}$	$\hat{4}$	$\hat{5}$	$\flat\hat{6}$	$\flat\hat{7}$	$\hat{1}$	$\hat{2}$
	G	A	B	C	D	E	F	G	A	B

Lydian

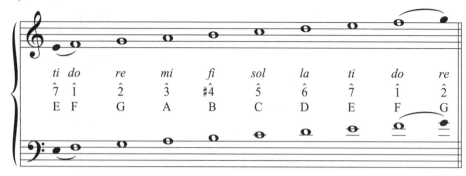

Phrygian

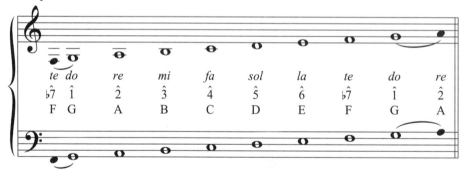

Mixolydian

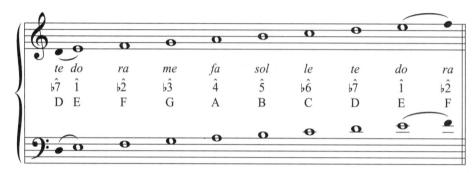

Lesson 5: Seventh Chords (Mm⁷, MM⁷, mm⁷) (Chapters 7ff.)

Choose a rhythm from Lesson 2, and improvise melodies that include the indicated seventh chord. Sing "sev" for $\hat{7}$. End on *do* ($\hat{1}$).

A. Mm⁷ as *sol–ti–re–fa* ($\hat{5}$–$\hat{7}$–$\hat{2}$–$\hat{4}$)

Sample solution with rhythm (1)

B. MM[7] as *do–mi–sol–ti* ($\hat{1}$–$\hat{3}$–$\hat{5}$–$\hat{7}$)

Sample solution with rhythm (3)

do do mi sol sol sol ti do ti do ti sol sol mi sol mi do mi do
$\hat{1}$ $\hat{1}$ $\hat{3}$ $\hat{5}$ $\hat{5}$ $\hat{5}$ $\hat{7}$ $\hat{1}$ $\hat{7}$ $\hat{1}$ $\hat{7}$ $\hat{5}$ $\hat{5}$ $\hat{3}$ $\hat{5}$ $\hat{3}$ $\hat{1}$ $\hat{3}$ $\hat{1}$

C. mm[7] as *re–fa–la–do* ($\hat{2}$–$\hat{4}$–$\hat{6}$–$\hat{1}$)

Sample solution with rhythm (2)

re fa la do do la do la do la fa la fa re fa re do
$\hat{2}$ $\hat{4}$ $\hat{6}$ $\hat{1}$ $\hat{1}$ $\hat{6}$ $\hat{1}$ $\hat{6}$ $\hat{1}$ $\hat{6}$ $\hat{4}$ $\hat{6}$ $\hat{4}$ $\hat{2}$ $\hat{4}$ $\hat{2}$ $\hat{1}$

D. Duet. Choose a rhythm from Lesson 2, and one type of seventh chord—Mm[7], MM[7], or mm[7]. Facing a partner, each person sings one measure in turn.

Lesson 6: First-Species Counterpoint (Chapter 9)

A. At the keyboard, play one of the cantus firmus (CF) fragments on the next page while singing one of its possible counterpoints to the right. Create a complete phrase by combining beginning, middle, and ending CF fragments while singing a corresponding contrapuntal line.

STRATEGIES

- Play each of the CFs, and memorize the counterpoints to train your ear to favor consonances (PU, 3rd, P5, 6th, and P8).

- Move in a variety of motions while avoiding parallel and direct perfect intervals.

B. While a partner sings a CF, improvise a first-species counterpoint by choosing from among the possible counterpoints to the right. Start with just the beginning fragments, then combine them with middle and ending fragments to create entire phrases. Switch parts and sing the CF for your partner.

C. Find a different partner who sings in a different range from your previous classmate; if you started each exercise on a unison before, find someone who sings an octave away from your part.

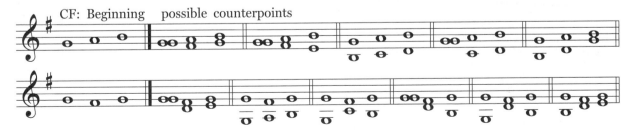

CF: Beginning   possible counterpoints

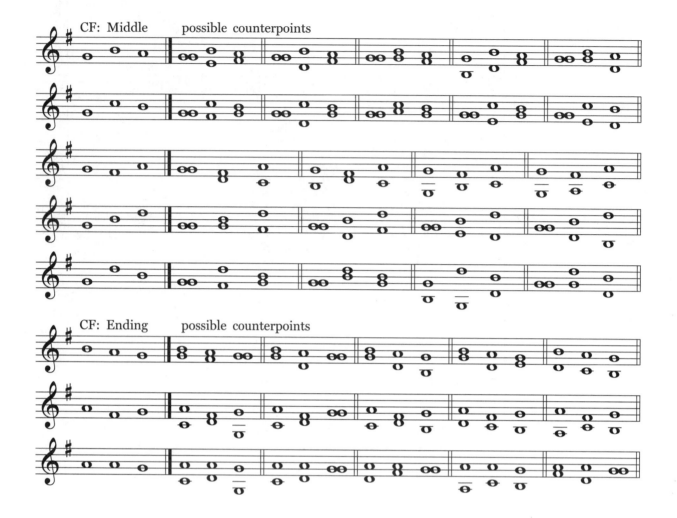

CF: Middle   possible counterpoints

CF: Ending   possible counterpoints

Lesson 7: Second-Species Counterpoint (Chapter 10)

Analyze the contrapuntal implications of the outline below by writing interval numbers between the staves. Then, with a partner, perform the outline as written. On the first repetition, embellish the higher part with consonant skips, passing tones, and/or neighbor tones. On the next repetition, embellish the lower part. Which suspensions may be created in mm. 3 and 7?

Other members of the class can critique the counterpoint by taking dictation, notating both the harmonic intervals and the melodic lines.

Lesson 8: Embellishing Melodic Outlines (Chapters 10, 16)

Improvise an embellished melody based on the outlines below. Add consonant skips, passing tones, neighbor tones, and rhythmic interest. Perform your improvisations in class. As you listen to the melodies of others, analyze the means by which the outline has been embellished—that is, where are the CS, P, and N?

STRATEGIES

- Begin by singing each part as written, then singing the melody while playing the bass line.
- Create études consisting of a single type of embellishment. For example, sing a variation that consists of nothing but skips within the chords. Sing another that features only upper neighbors, one that features lower neighbors, etc.
- Improvise melodies that combine ideas from your études into new, original music.

Outline 1 (Compare with Joseph Haydn, Piano Sonata No. 15 in C Major, Minuet.)

Outline 2 (Compare with the traditional song "Good Night Ladies.")

VARIATIONS

- Improvise in the parallel minor keys, and include the leading tone.
- Transpose the outline to major and minor keys from three flats to three sharps.
- Perform the improvisation as a duet, one person per staff.
- The class sustains the pitches of the outline while one or two performers improvise.

Lesson 9: Improvising Melodies in Phrase Pairs (Chapters 12ff.)

Improvise a melody that may be accompanied by each progression below. Sing the melody while accompanying yourself at the keyboard. Direct the melody of each phrase toward the cadence, ideally descending to *re* (2̂) at the first cadence (m. 4) and *do* (1̂) at the second cadence. Follow the strategies from Lesson 8.

Progression 1

Progression 2

Duet 1: While one person plays an embellished version of progression 1 or 2, the partner improvises a melody by singing or playing an instrument. Switch roles and perform again.
Duet 2: Work with a partner to improvise a two-phrase melody. One person creates a phrase that leads to a half cadence, descending to *re* (2̂). The partner begins phrase 2 with phrase 1's motive, but ends with a PAC, descending to *do* (1̂). Each performer should prepare to be both leader and follower. Perform in both major and minor keys, in both $\frac{4}{4}$ and $\frac{6}{8}$.

STRATEGIES FOR TEAM IMPROVISATION

- Create motives that are simple and memorable so followers can recall them easily.
- Organize phrases with a sentence structure: a one-bar idea followed by a one-bar variation of the idea, then a two-bar contrasting idea that leads to the cadence.
- Make your melodic lines rise so they will be able to descend to the cadence. Cadence on a strong beat.
- Use mostly stepwise motion. Make skips part of tonic or dominant triads.
- If singing, conduct as you perform.
- Draw empty measures on the board or overhead projector. Plan which measures will contain which harmonic ideas.

Lesson 10: Improvising over Figured Basses and Roman Numeral Progressions (Chapters 14–15)

Practice realizing the short preparatory exercises below (A (1) and B (1)), then incorporate them into the progression that follows (A (2) and B (2)). Use voice-leading identical to that of Keyboard Lessons 8, 10, and 11. Play the realized progression, singing a melodic variation of an upper part. Perform again, basing your improvisation on a different part. Follow the strategies from Lesson 8.

A. (1) Major-key preparation

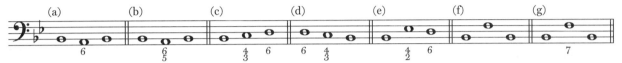

(2) Figured-bass progression 1

B. (1) Minor-key preparation

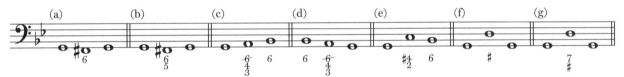

(2) Figured-bass progression 2

Duet: While one person realizes a progression below, another improvises a melody.

Phrase 1
(a) I–vi–ii^6–V$^{8-7}_{6-3}_{4-3}$

(b) I–IV^6–I^6–IV–V$^{8-7}_{6-3}_{4-3}$

Phrase 2
I–vi–ii^6–V$^{8-7}_{6-3}_{4-3}$–I

I–IV^6–I^6–IV–V$^{8-7}_{6-3}_{4-3}$–I

To the strategies from Lesson 8 add the following.

- Use voice-leading identical to that of keyboard Lessons 9 A and 12 C.
- Animate the texture of the accompaniment: for example, arpeggiate chords instead of playing block harmonies.
- Listen for problems, such as parallel octaves or fifths between solo and accompaniment, and correct them.
- Perform each progression in its parallel minor key.

Lesson 11: Conclusive and Inconclusive Phrases (Chapters 12ff.)

A. Conclusive phrases: The melodies below end with a HC. Perform each melody, then improvise a second phrase based on the melodic idea of the first. Conclude your new phrase with a PAC.

Amy Beach, "Forgotten"

Johannes Brahms, Clarinet Quintet, Op. 115, third movement

Hugo Wolf, "Das verlassene Mägdlein" ("The Abandoned Maiden")

B. Inconclusive phrases: The melodies below end with authentic cadences. Improvise a phrase that *precedes* each melody, concluding with a HC. Perform your phrase, then the given melody.

Johann Sebastian Bach, *Partita No. 1*, Bourrée

Fanny Mendelssohn Hensel, "Beharre"

Louise Farrenc, Trio in E Minor, Op. 45

Lesson 12: Improvising with Predominant Chords (Chapters 14–15)

While one person plays the accompaniments below, everyone else takes turns improvising a melody. Choose a part and embellish it, following the strategies from Lesson 8. Before anyone sings aloud, have someone play the progression several times while the class silently improvises. Make sure each person accompanies as well as performs a melody.

Progression 1

Progression 2

VARIATIONS

- Begin with four-measure solos. Later, extend them to eight or sixteen measures, or shorten them to two measures.
- Swap "fours." One person improvises four bars, then a second responds to the first improvisation.
- Try a variety of styles (art song, pop song, jazz, and so on). Create rhythmic embellishments in the accompaniment that are characteristic of the chosen style. Change the tempo, mood, and character to reflect the chosen style.
- Perform each example in its parallel-minor mode.
- Transpose the examples to keys ranging from three flats to three sharps.
- Change the meters to compound meters.
- Transcribe the examples for instruments available in class. Play the accompaniment on those instruments. Let each player improvise within his or her part.
- Create a "groove" by adding one or more percussionists who play instruments available in class (books, desktops, pencils, etc.).

Lesson 13: Improvising Periods (Chapters 18ff.)

Following the procedures from Lesson 9, work with a partner to improvise a melody that creates each of the following structures: parallel period, contrasting period, parallel double period, contrasting double period.

Lesson 14: Improvising Sequences (Chapters 19ff.)

Use each sequence below as the basis for improvisations. Play the outline at the keyboard while singing an improvised melody, or improvise on your instrument while someone accompanies you, improvising at the keyboard.

STRATEGIES

- Because the patterns are sequential, think of a motive that you can perform over a two-chord segment. Then transpose this pattern down to the next segment.
- Compound melodies work beautifully over these sequences. Create motives that imply two melodic strands.
- Follow the strategies from Lesson 8.

Sequence 1

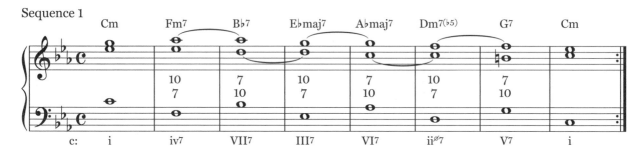

Sequence 2

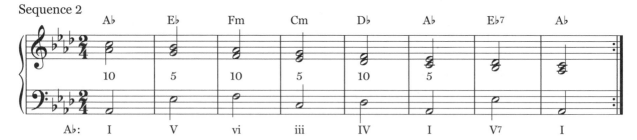

VARIATIONS

Keyboard Lessons 14–15 show ways to prepare the last four bulleted items.

- Change to triple meter.
- Change to compound meter.
- Perform each sequence in its parallel minor key.
- Add melodic embellishments, such as suspensions (e.g., in sequence 2: I–V$^{4-3}$–vi$^{9-8}$–iii$^{4-3}$, etc.).
- Chromaticize the sequence.
- Assign the given soprano voice to a different part to create a different linear intervallic pattern (LIP).
- Change the inversions of the chords (e.g., in sequence 1: i–iv^6–VII–III^6, etc.).

Lesson 15: Phrase Expansion, Asymmetrical Meter, and Tonicization (Chapters 18, 20–21)

Improvise a melody while a partner plays the following lullaby, then switch roles. Model your voice-leading on the voice-leading in the accompaniment. Conduct whenever you sing your improvisation.

STRATEGIES

- First perform the rhythm only, tapping the bass part in your left hand and the treble part in your right. Switch hands and perform again.
- Initially, play the chords as block chords; then apply the rhythm.
- Singers should conduct in an asymmetric duple meter (3+2).

Joel Phillips, *Lullaby*

Variations: Transcribe the accompaniment for guitar and perform again. Improvise an introduction in the style of the piece. Improvise a codetta in the style of the piece.

Lesson 16: Modulatory Periods (Chapters 22ff.)

At the keyboard, improvise modulatory periods in both major and minor keys following the plans below.

Keyboard Lesson 17 shows how to create phrases that modulate. To make phrase 1, which concludes with a half cadence, select one of the following progressions.

- Keyboard Lesson 12 C (1): stop at chord 4b.
- Keyboard Lesson 12 C (2): stop at chord 5b.
- Keyboard Lesson 13 B (1) (minor keys only).

To make phrase 2, transpose Keyboard Lesson 12 C (1) or (2) to the related key—V in major or III in minor.

VARIATIONS

- Animate the texture, playing arpeggios, a "boom-chick" rhythm, and so on.
- Embellish your improvisation with passing tones, neighbor tones, suspensions, and consonant skips.
- Play a simple accompaniment while improvising a melody.
- One person improvises an accompaniment while another improvises a melody.
- Begin phrase 2 with a different progression, such as that from Keyboard Lesson 9 A.
- Create your own key-defining progression.

Lesson 17: Mixture, Phrase Expansion, A⁶ and N⁶ Chords (Chapters 25–26)

A. Improvise a waltz from the melodic and harmonic outline below. While one person realizes the figured bass at the keyboard, another improvises a melody. Sing with solfège syllables and scale-degree numbers that reflect the modal mixture.

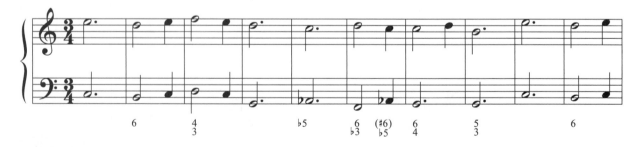

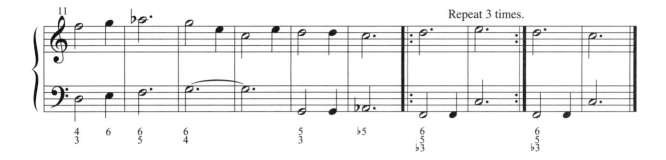

Beat 3 of m. 6 may be performed two ways. Until you learn A⁶ chords, ignore the parenthetical figure and perform only the ♭5. Once you learn A⁶ chords, perform both figures— the parenthetical ♯6 and the ♭5.

B. Write the correct Roman numerals in the blanks below the bass pitches, then improvise an accompaniment to this waltz while a second performer improvises a melody, singing with solfège syllables or scale-degree numbers.

VARIATIONS

- Animate the texture of the accompaniment. For example, arpeggiate the chords instead of playing them as block harmonies.
- Once you have analyzed the chords, perform looking only the Roman numerals.
- Create a different type of dance by changing the meter to simple quadruple.

Lesson 18: Blues and Rock (Chapters 28ff.)

A. Blues: While one performer realizes the chords of the twelve-bar blues on keyboard or guitar, a soloist improvises, drawing on pitches of the blues scale. Switch roles and perform again. Soloists may sing their improvisations or play them on an instrument.

To get started, review the C blues scale and progression found in Keyboard Lesson 19. On your DVD, locate the audio files "C blues.mp3" and "F blues.mp3" (in the "Part III

Improvisation" folder). On your own, listen to these accompaniments and practice singing your improvisation.

Variations: Transpose the blues scale and progression to the key of F. Ask multiple soloists to improvise over the accompaniment. The first performs a four-measure motive based on the blues scale. A second imitates the motive, adjusting for the chord change. The third makes a variation of the motive that cadences in m. 11.

B. Rock: Take the progression below as the basis for the verse of a song in a classic rock style. Embellish the outline as you sing an improvisation.

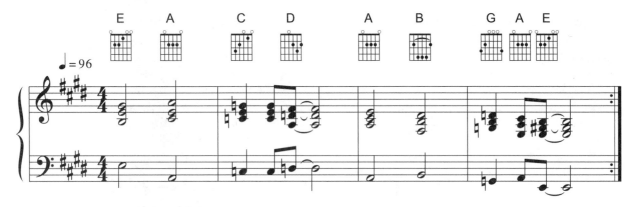

On your DVD, find the audio file "Rock.mp3." On your own, listen to this accompaniment and practice singing your improvisation.

VARIATIONS

- Accompany yourself on keyboard or guitar.
- Initially, play the music as written. Later, embellish the rhythm, but keep a steady, driving beat.
- Add other instruments, like percussion and bass, to create an ensemble.
- Make a quintet of singers. While four people sing the progression, a fifth improvises a melody. Swap parts each time, so each person has a chance to improvise.
- Improvise a chorus, then perform ‖: verse, verse, chorus :‖.

Lesson 19: Ragtime (Chapters 29ff.)

While one person plays a ragtime accompaniment based on the outline below, a second improvises a melody. The accompanist should also improvise, embellishing the outline and imitating the soloist when possible. Each performer should prepare to solo or accompany.

On your DVD, find the audio file "Ragtime.mp3." On your own, listen to this accompaniment and practice singing your improvisation.

STRATEGIES

- According to Scott Joplin, rags should never be played fast. Try a nice strolling tempo of around MM = 72.

- Create a motive that features rhythms characteristic of rags, such as these four:

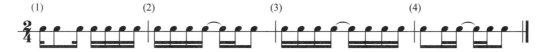

- Perform the motive each time the opening chord progression recurs. Transform the motive in other places.

- In m. 8, one or both performers should create a lead-in to the next phrase. (The bass is a good place to play the lead-in!)

Lesson 20: Continuous Variations (Chapters 31ff.)

Improvise a series of continuous variations based on the "Lament" below. On your DVD, locate the audio file "Lament.mp3." On your own, listen to this accompaniment and practice singing your improvisation.

- *Solos:* Play the outer voices at the keyboard, and improvise a melody. Sing with solfège syllables or scale-degree numbers.

- *Duets:* One person improvises a keyboard accompaniment from the outline while the other improvises a melody. Switch parts and perform again.

- *Trios:* Three instrumentalists improvise a line based on one of the parts. On each repetition, switch parts until each performer has improvised on each part.

Very slow and expressive

e: i   10-10 LIP ——————————————————————— V   VI ii°^{6} V i

To shape your performance: Perform the bass line by itself. Then on the first repetition, sing a simple melody in counterpoint. On each successive repetition, make your melody increasingly elaborate. After your most elaborate embellishment, recapitulate the simple (first) melody as the last variation.

Lesson 21: Modes and Scales (Chapters 33ff.)

Following the guidelines below, create an **additive** *crescendo* and a **subtractive** *diminuendo*.

1. Choose one of the following collections: a mode, the pentatonic scale, the octatonic scale, the whole-tone scale, or a scale of your own. Perform it to get the sounds in your ears, voice, and fingers. Remember, members of the scale are pitch classes and may be expressed in any octave.

2. Begin quietly with a brief motivic idea, based on your chosen collection, which may be repeated and varied throughout. A second person then enters, performing an idea that in some way complements the first. (This second idea might be contrasting in rhythm, register, timbre, articulation, etc.) Other performers likewise enter one at a time until the texture is dense and the dynamics loud.

3. At the dynamic peak, a soloist joins the texture, singing or playing a slow, lyrical melodic line that will sharply contrast with the more chaotic background.

4. Gradually the ensemble reduces its dynamics, and performers drop out one by one.

5. The soloist concludes the improvisation with a brief cadenza.

VARIATIONS

• Before performing, decide on a word that describes the general character or mood of the improvisation (e.g., "frightening," "joyful," "melancholic"). Craft your improvisations to reflect this character.

• At the high point, point to a new scale. As seamlessly as possible, perform the same melodic shapes, but now with the pcs of the new collection.

• Choose one scale, switch to a second, and return to the first to create an **A B A** design.

• When the texture is full, listen for a specific performer. Create a call and response between yourself and that performer.

• Record your improvisations. Listen to the performances and analyze what you hear. Do you hear any "wrong" notes (i.e., notes not in the scale)? Who played them? Are there parts that turned out especially well? Transcribe them to see why they were successful. Consider using some of these ideas in your compositions.

Lesson 22: Whole-Tone and Pentatonic Scales (Chapters 34ff.)

Improvise an **A B A** duet that moves from whole-tone sets to pentatonic sets, then back to whole-tone sets. Choose from the sets below, moving from one set to the next by means of the "pivot" trichord { 6 8 t }. On your own, practice singing and playing the sets. Remember that you may realize the pitch classes in any octave.

Whole-tone sets: {6 8 t}, {6 8 0}, {6 t 4}, {6 8 t 0}, {6 8 t 2}, {6 8 0 2}
Pentatonic sets:　{1 3 6}, {1 3 8}, {6 8 t}, {1 3 6 8}, {6 8 t 1 3}
"Pivot set" to move between collections: {6 8 t }

- Let one performer develop an ostinato based on one of the whole-tone sets.
- A second performer improvises a melody based on any of the remaining whole-tone sets.
- At a predetermined signal, such as a nod of the head, both perform only pcs from the "pivot" collection {6 8 t}.
- At a second signal, they move to the pentatonic sets and repeat the process (with one improvising an ostinato and the other a melody).
- Return to the whole-tone sets, again by means of {6 8 t}.

VARIATIONS

- Add percussion to the ensemble with classroom objects such as pencils on notebooks, hand tapping, etc.
- Add a conductor. The performers must follow the gestures of the conductor, adjusting elements of their performance such as dynamics, tempo, and texture.

Lesson 23: Octatonic Scales and Subsets (Chapters 35ff.)

Choose one of the set classes below and realize it as pitches on the board. Write its transpositions and inversions as well. Add to this each of the three distinct versions of the octatonic scale (for example, scales beginning whole step / half step, that include the pc C, C♯, or D). Perform all these examples to get the sounds in your ears, voice, and fingers. Remember to think of these realizations as pitch classes that may be expressed in any octave.

4-3 [0 1 3 4]　4-9 [0 1 6 7]　4-Z15 [0 1 4 6]　5-28 [0 2 3 6 8]　5-31 [0 1 3 6 9]

- Let one performer develop an ostinato based on some version of the set.
- A second performer improvises a melody based on the octatonic scale that contains the pitches of the ostinato.
- If the accompanist changes to a different transposition or inversion of the set, the improviser should hear the change and adjust to a new octatonic scale.

- Relying on a predetermined signal, such as a nod of the head, the performers should switch their roles in the middle of the improvisation. Switch once more to give the improvisation an **A B A** design.
- Add percussion to the ensemble, improvising with classroom objects. Listen to the melodic improviser and try to create a rhythmic canon.
- Add a second melodic improviser who must imitate the first improviser's melody, but in inversion, and feature pcs from the same octatonic scale.
- Add a conductor. The performers must follow the gestures of the conductor, adjusting elements of their performance such as dynamics, tempo, and texture.
- Add a speaker. The speaker might recite poetry or interject familiar maxims from musical history, such as Fux's "*Mi* contra *fa* est diabolus in musica" from *Gradus ad Parnassum*. (Today we might say, "The tritone is the devil in music.")

Lesson 24: Twelve-Tone Dance (Chapters 36ff.)

Choose a row from the "Contextual Listening" or "Sight-Singing," sections, or create one of your own. Select at least two forms of the row to use in an improvisation—a short dance movement—that you will perform on a pitched instrument of your choice. Notate your choices of row form on the board. Select one of the dance rhythms below for the motivic rhythm of your improvisation.

- Practice the row forms and the rhythm separately before putting them together.
- Remember, these are pcs, so practice them in every octave available on your instrument.
- Practice expressing the intervals in both conjunct and disjunct lines. Many twelve-tone melodies express each interval in the series as a leap.

VARIATIONS

- Create your own dance rhythms.
- Choose row forms that lend themselves to overlaps. See if your classmates can hear where these overlaps occur.
- Create a matrix from your row, and thread your way through one or more forms each of P, I, R, and RI.
- Ask a friend to listen to your improvisation, then play a canon along with you.

Lesson 25: Polymetric Duets (Chapters 38ff.)

Create a polymetric ostinato. First, take two meters, $\frac{3}{4}$ and $\frac{4}{4}$, and multiply their beats (the top number in the signature): multiply 3 times 4. Your ostinato will be twelve *beats* long—four measures of 3 and three measures of 4, heard at the same time.

- Performer 1 begins by improvising a four-measure rhythmic ostinato in $\frac{3}{4}$ meter.
- Once the ostinato is established, performer 2 enters, improvising a three-measure ostinato in $\frac{4}{4}$ as the first performer continues.
- To make the meters more audible, each person should choose a contrasting timbre, choose rhythmic patterns common to the meters, and emphasize the metric accent.
- Following the same procedure, combine other meters.

Part I Keyboard Lessons

When studying this chapter,	review Lesson(s)	then complete Lesson(s)
3		1
4	1	
5	1	2, 3
6	2, 3	4
7		5
8	5	6
9		7
10	1–7	

Lesson 1: Major Pentachords, Tetrachords, and Scales (Chapter 3)

For all exercises that follow, sing with note names, solfège syllables, and scale-degree numbers as you play up and down the patterns.

C major pentachord with right- and left-hand fingering

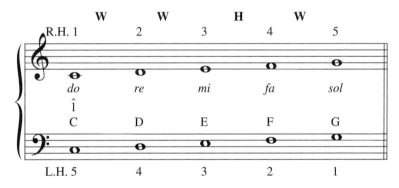

C major scale constructed from two major tetrachords (C major tetrachord + G major tetrachord)

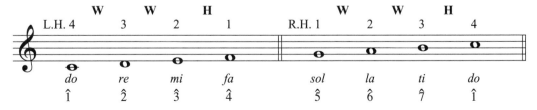

A. Play major pentachords in octaves with both hands from the starting pitches listed below.

(1) A	(5) F♯	(9) B♭	*Musical challenges!*
(2) F	(6) E	(10) B	(13) A♯
(3) G	(7) C♯	(11) G♭	(14) D♯
(4) E♭	(8) A♭	(12) D♭	(15) F♭

B. Beginning on the starting pitches listed in exercise A, play major tetrachords in octaves with both hands.

C. Play an ascending major scale starting from each of the following tonic pitches. As you play each pitch, sing its name.

(1) D	(5) E♭	(9) E	*Musical challenges!*
(2) F	(6) F♯/G♭	(10) G	(13) G♯
(3) A♭	(7) A	(11) B♭	(14) F♭
(4) B/C♭	(8) C	(12) D♭/C♯	(15) D♯

Lesson 2: Minor Pentachords, Tetrachords, and Scales (Chapter 5)

C minor pentachord with right- and left-hand fingering

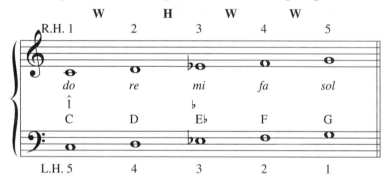

To make the minor tetrachord, perform the first four notes of the minor pentachord.

Natural minor scale (the same notes found in the minor key signature)

Harmonic minor scale (Look at the minor key signature, and raise ♭$\hat{7}$.)

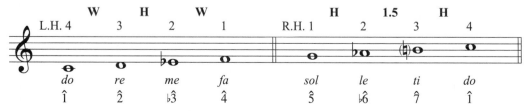

Ascending melodic minor scale (Play a major scale, but lower $\hat{3}$ a half step; or look at the minor key signature, and raise $\flat\hat{6}$ and $\flat\hat{7}$.)

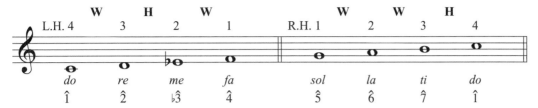

Descending melodic minor scale (same as natural minor)

A. Play minor pentachords in octaves with both hands from the starting pitches listed in Lesson 1 A. Play minor tetrachords from the same pitches.

B. From each pitch in Lesson 1 A, play the natural, harmonic, and melodic minor scale, ascending and descending.

Lesson 3: Diatonic Modes (Chapter 5)

You already know two diatonic modes: the major mode, also called the Ionian mode; and the natural (descending melodic) minor mode, also called the Aeolian mode. Below are the remaining common diatonic modes with two different ways to remember them.

Dorian mode

Perform a natural minor scale and raise $\flat\hat{6}$ a half step.

Call the first pitch *re* ($\hat{2}$). Perform a major scale from *re* to *re* ($\hat{2}$–$\hat{2}$).

Phrygian mode

Perform a natural minor scale and lower $\hat{2}$ a half step (sung *ra*).

Call the first pitch *mi* ($\hat{3}$). Perform a major scale from *mi* to *mi* ($\hat{3}$–$\hat{3}$).

Lydian mode

Perform a major scale and raise $\hat{4}$ a half step (sung *fi*).

Call the first pitch *fa* ($\hat{4}$). Perform a major scale from *fa* to *fa* ($\hat{4}$–$\hat{4}$).

Mixolydian mode

Perform a major scale and lower
$\hat{7}$ a half step (sung *te*).

Call the first pitch *sol* ($\hat{5}$). Perform a major scale
from *sol* to *sol* ($\hat{5}$–$\hat{5}$).

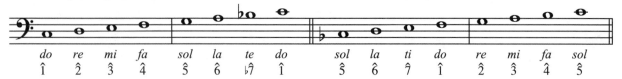

do	*re*	*mi*	*fa*	*sol*	*la*	*te*	*do*	*sol*	*la*	*ti*	*do*	*re*	*mi*	*fa*	*sol*
$\hat{1}$	$\hat{2}$	$\hat{3}$	$\hat{4}$	$\hat{5}$	$\hat{6}$	$\flat\hat{7}$	$\hat{1}$	$\hat{5}$	$\hat{6}$	$\hat{7}$	$\hat{1}$	$\hat{2}$	$\hat{3}$	$\hat{4}$	$\hat{5}$

Beginning on the given pitch, play the mode specified, ascending and descending.

(1) D Dorian
(4) B Phrygian
(7) A Lydian
(10) G Mixolydian

(2) F Mixolydian
(5) B♭ Lydian
(8) D Mixolydian
(11) B♭ Ionian

(3) G♯ Aeolian
(6) F♯ Phrygian
(9) E♭ Lydian
(12) E Dorian

Lesson 4: Intervals (Chapter 6)

A. Intervals from the major scale and the Phrygian mode

Sing the entire scale or mode below, then each interval above and below C as shown.
Perform each interval four times, singing with solfège syllables, scale-degree numbers,
note names, and interval names. (For example: "*do–do*, 1–$\hat{1}$, C–C, perfect unison"; "*do–re*,
$\hat{1}$–$\hat{2}$, C–D, major second"; etc.)

C major scale: Major and perfect intervals above C, minor and perfect intervals below C

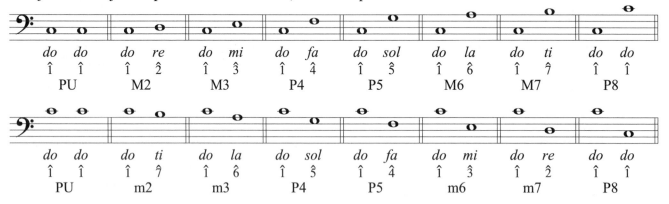

C Phrygian mode: Minor and perfect intervals above C, major and perfect intervals below C

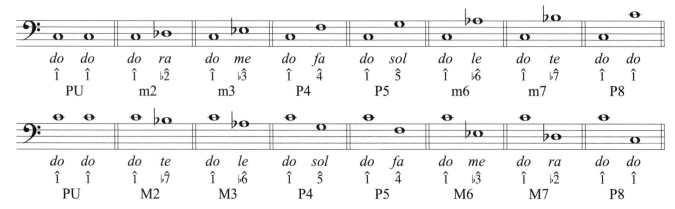

Imagine the given pitch to be the lowest or highest note of either a major scale or Phrygian mode, as in exercise A. Sing up or down with solfège syllables, scale-degree numbers, letter names, and interval names until you reach the interval specified. Play the two notes of the interval simultaneously as a harmony. Then play the lower pitch and sing the higher one; switch and play the higher pitch and sing the lower.

B. Ascending major and perfect intervals

(1) M6 above D	(5) P5 above B♭	(9) M3 above G♭	(13) M2 above F
(2) M2 above A♭	(6) P4 above B	(10) P8 above G	(14) P4 above F
(3) M3 above F♯	(7) M7 above E♭	(11) M3 above A	(15) M6 above B
(4) M7 above D♭	(8) M6 above C♯	(12) P5 above A♭	(16) M3 above C♯

C. Descending minor and perfect intervals

(1) m2 below A	(5) m2 below B♭	(9) m6 below E	(13) m3 below C♯
(2) m2 below C♯	(6) P4 below D♭	(10) m3 below F	(14) P4 below B♭
(3) P8 below A♯	(7) m7 below B	(11) m3 below A♭	(15) P5 below A
(4) m7 below E♭	(8) m3 below F♯	(12) P5 below F	(16) m6 below D

D. Ascending minor and perfect intervals

(1) m3 above E	(5) m2 above C♯	(9) m2 above A	(13) m3 above G♯
(2) P5 above B	(6) m6 above B♭	(10) m3 above F♯	(14) m7 above D
(3) m2 above D	(7) P4 above F	(11) m7 above A♭	(15) m6 above F
(4) m6 above A	(8) m7 above E♭	(12) P5 above D♭	(16) m3 above E♭

E. Descending major and perfect intervals

(1) M2 below D	(5) M2 below D♭	(9) M6 below E	(13) M3 below C♯
(2) M6 below E♭	(6) P4 below G	(10) M3 below F	(14) M6 below B♭
(3) M3 below B♭	(7) M7 below B	(11) M3 below A♭	(15) M2 below A
(4) M7 below F♯	(8) M3 below F♯	(12) P5 below C	(16) M7 below E

F. Ascending and descending major, minor, and perfect intervals
Beginning on G, E, D♭, B, and G♭, play and sing all the following intervals.

(1) M6 above	(5) m7 above	(9) P4 above	(13) m2 above
(2) M3 below	(6) m6 below	(10) m7 below	(14) P4 below
(3) P5 above	(7) M7 above	(11) M3 above	(15) M2 below
(4) m2 below	(8) P5 below	(12) M7 below	(16) m7 above E

G. Augmented and diminished intervals

(1) Augment the following perfect and major intervals.

- Play the given interval, then raise the upper pitch a half step; name the new interval.
- Play the given interval again, then lower the bottom pitch a half step; name the new interval.

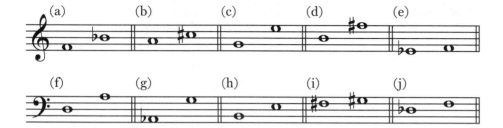

(2) Diminish the following perfect and minor intervals.

- Play the given interval, then lower the upper pitch a half step; name the new interval.
- Play the given interval again, then raise the bottom pitch a half step; name the new interval.

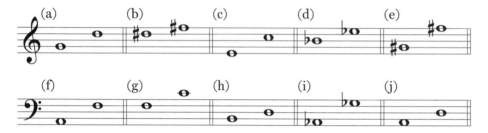

Lesson 5: Triads (Chapter 7)

A. Major and minor triads

From each tonic pitch below, perform a major pentachord and triad, then a minor pentachord and triad. The triad is the first, third, and fifth notes of the pentachord. Perform the patterns in both simple and compound meters.

- Recall the key signature associated with each tonic pitch.
- Play the patterns in both hands simultaneously.
- Sing with solfège syllables, scale-degree numbers, and letter names.

(1) G	(5) E♭	(9) E	*Musical challenges!*
(2) F	(6) C♯	(10) B♭	(13) A♯
(3) A♭	(7) A	(11) F♯	(14) G♯
(4) B	(8) C	(12) G♭	(15) D♯

B. Augmented and diminished triads

(1) From each pitch given in exercise A, perform a major triad, then *raise the fifth* a half step to create an augmented triad. Finally, resolve the augmented fifth up a half step. If you sing the first pitch as *do* (1̂), hear how the augmented fifth lies between *sol* and *la* (5̂ and 6̂).

(2) From each pitch in exercise A, perform a minor triad. Then *lower the fifth* a half step to create a diminished triad.

(3) Diminished triads in minor-key music: We hear the diminished triad as the supertonic chord in minor keys and as the leading-tone chord in both major and minor keys. Sing the example below to hear how the pitches of a diminished fifth resolve toward each other into a third.

Example: The given tonic is B.

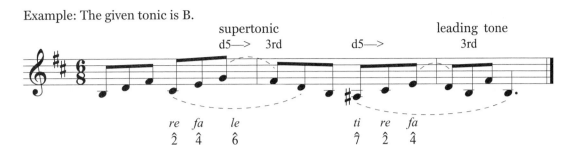

Transpose the example above to begin on A, E, G, C♯, and F. Sing with solfège syllables, scale-degree numbers, and letter names.

Lesson 6: Seventh Chords (Chapter 8)

From each of the roots E, A, C, F♯, and G, play a major triad with the root doubled at the octave. Then lower one chord note at a time to create all five common seventh chords on the root.

Example: The root is B.

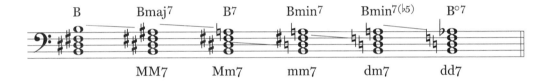

Lesson 7: Counterpoint (Chapters 10–11)

A. Note-to-note species counterpoint

(1) Harmonize a melody with imperfect consonances.

(a) First, play and sing the melody.

(b) Next, play the melody while singing thirds below it.

(c) This time, play the melody while singing sixths below it.

(2) For lines to be truly contrapuntal, they must sometimes move *with* the melody and other times *against* it, so that the parts will sound independent of each other. Mix the thirds and sixths this time, and add a few perfect consonances (PU, P5, or P8). These

may also appear in the middle of phrases, but not as often as thirds and sixths, and never in succession.

U   3   3   6   6   3   3   6   5   6

(3) Follow all the same steps to harmonize, and add counterpoint to the melody below. Remember to employ pitches from the melodic minor scale, raising $\flat\hat{6}$ and $\flat\hat{7}$ when ascending and lowering $\hat{6}$ and $\hat{7}$ when descending.

B. Second-species counterpoint: Passing tones, neighbor tones, and consonant skips and steps

(1) Perform each first-species exercise below, (a)–(c), as written. Sing one part while playing the other, then switch parts.

(2) Convert each exercise to second species by replacing the half notes in the higher part with two quarter notes. The first quarter must be the same pitch as the half note it replaces.

Try the following embellishments in the counterpoint wherever possible, and choose the ones that sound best.

- a passing tone placed between skips
- a neighbor tone added between repeated notes
- a consonant skip or step (CS) added between steps

First-species example

One possible second-species solution

(a)

(b)

(c)

C. Performing suspensions

(1) Perform the consonant sixths below, then the displaced sixths (shown with arrows) to hear 7–6 suspensions. Note that the dissonance (7) occurs on the strong part of the beat and the resolution (6) on the weak part.

Consonant sixths

Displaced sixths become 7–6 suspensions.

(2) In a series of thirds, either the upper or lower part may be displaced (shown with arrows). A delayed upper part creates 4–3 suspensions; a delayed lower part creates 2–3 (bass) suspensions. Perform the consonant thirds, then each type of suspension. Again, the dissonance (4 or 2) occurs on the strong part of the beat and the consonance (3) on the weak part.

Consonant thirds

Displaced upper part becomes a chain of 4–3 suspensions.

Displaced lower part becomes a chain of 2–3 (bass) suspensions.

(3) Taking exercises (1) and (2) above as models, embellish the music below to include suspensions when possible. The 2–3 suspension may occur only in the lower part,

but the other suspensions may occur in either part. Play the original twice, singing first the lower part, then the upper. Next, play the lower part while singing the upper. Finally, sing the lower part while playing the upper.

The keyboard lessons for Parts II and III, covering materials from Chapters 11–32, are organized in a way that will facilitate spiral learning. As you proceed through *The Musician's Guide,* you may initially want to complete only part(s) of a certain lesson and skip other parts. Then when a chapter introduces a new concept, return to that earlier lesson, review it, and complete the part(s) you skipped initially. Connecting a new concept to one you already know will help you understand how the new is merely a variation of the old. When you have completed these lessons, you will understand that they consolidate essential aspects of tonal harmony and, as such, will be excellent review and preparation for taking graduate placement examinations.

Parts II–III Keyboard Lessons

When studying this chapter,	review Lesson(s)	then complete Lesson(s)
11		8 A
12	8 A	8 B
13	8 A & B	9 A, 10 A
14	9 A, 10 A	11 A & B, 12 A & B
15	8 A & B, 9 A	12 C & D, 13 A, 13 B (1)
16	8 A, 11 A	14
17	10 A, 12 C	10 B
18	8–14	
19		15 A (1), 15 B (1), 15 C (1), 15 D (1)
20	10 A	16 A
21	10 A & B, 16 A	16 B & C

When studying this chapter,	review Lesson(s)	then complete Lesson(s)
22	9 A, 12 C, 15 A (1)	17
23	9 A, 12 C, 15 B (1), 17	
24	9 A, 12 C, 15 D (1), 17	
25		18
26	9 A, 13 B (1)	9 B, 13 B (2)
27	9 B, 13 B (2)	
28		19
29		20, all of 15
30–32	15–20	

Lessons 8–20 will help you develop a practical understanding of four-part harmony by playing, singing, and memorizing short progressions that are the essence of tonal music. Some progressions may be correctly realized in other ways, but by memorizing the most common realizations, you will have a basis for comparison with alternate methods.

Always perform all examples, singing with solfège syllables, scale-degree numbers, and/or letter names.

- Sing the bass line.
- Play the bass line and sing each of the upper voices with it.
- Play the bass line, play *two* upper voices, and sing the remaining part.
- Play all four parts four times, singing a different part each time.

Memorize the parts, singing the voice-leading as melody to help you. Apply the voice-leading to solving musical problems.

Practice the progressions: play in both major and minor keys, ranging from three sharps to three flats; notate what you play. Include the model progressions as the basis of making your own music—both improvisations and compositions. Listen to and look at musical literature to find how these progressions are featured and how they are varied.

Solfège and scale-degree grids: Because syllables and numbers help us generalize musical patterns, solfège and scale-degree grids are provided in the following lessons so that you can easily memorize the progressions. In most grids, the bass part is constant. The other melodic lines are called parts 1, 2, and 3—each might appear in the soprano, alto, or tenor voice.

Look at Lesson 8 A. Example 1's soprano voice is *mi–re–do* ($\hat{3}$–$\hat{2}$–$\hat{1}$), part 1 in the grids below. In example 2, part 1 appears in the alto voice and in example 3 in the tenor voice. Note that in example 3, part 2 (*do–ti–sol*, originally in the alto) changes. That is because when *ti* ($\hat{7}$) appears in an outer voice, it *must* rise to *do* ($\hat{1}$). Though the melodies of these parts remain intact most of the time, they can change for such important reasons.

Lesson 8: The Basic Phrase: Tonic- and Dominant-Function Chords (Chapters 11ff.)

Learn the models below, then perform them in major and minor keys from three flats to three sharps. For the V triad, omit the parenthetical seventh and sustain *sol* ($\hat{5}$); for V7, include it.

A. I–V$^{(8-7)}$–I

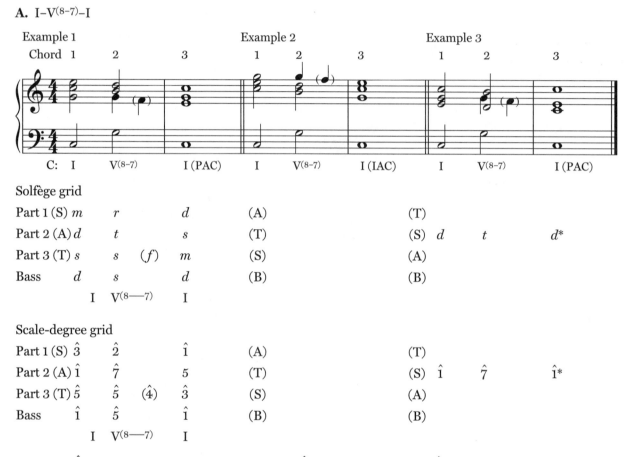

Solfège grid

Part 1 (S)	*m*	*r*		*d*	(A)			(T)			
Part 2 (A)	*d*	*t*		*s*	(T)			(S)	*d*	*t*	*d**
Part 3 (T)	*s*	*s*	(*f*)	*m*	(S)			(A)			
Bass	*d*	*s*		*d*	(B)			(B)			
		I	V$^{(8——7)}$	I							

Scale-degree grid

Part 1 (S)	$\hat{3}$	$\hat{2}$		$\hat{1}$	(A)			(T)			
Part 2 (A)	$\hat{1}$	$\hat{7}$		5	(T)			(S)	$\hat{1}$	$\hat{7}$	$\hat{1}$*
Part 3 (T)	$\hat{5}$	$\hat{5}$	($\hat{4}$)	$\hat{3}$	(S)			(A)			
Bass	$\hat{1}$	$\hat{5}$		$\hat{1}$	(B)			(B)			
		I	V$^{(8——7)}$	I							

*When *ti* ($\hat{7}$) is in an outer voice, it must rise to *do* ($\hat{1}$). In an inner voice, *ti* ($\hat{7}$) may fall to *sol* ($\hat{5}$).

Authentic and half cadence: Chords 2–3 create an authentic cadence (AC). If *do* ($\hat{1}$) occurs in the soprano of chord 3, the cadence is perfect authentic (PAC); if not, the cadence is imperfect authentic (IAC). Chords 1–2 create a half cadence (HC); for half cadences, exclude the seventh from V.

To help you memorize the voice-leading, combine all four parts into a melody, as shown below. Feel free to change the rhythm, and sing parts where they fit comfortably within your own voice's range.

Grid sung as melody (sample realization)

Bass _____   Part 1 _____   Part 2 _____   Part 3 _____

Now apply this strategy to solve the following problems.

(1) In D major, realize the progression I–V$^{8-7}$–I in four voices, SATB.

Sing the progression's melody, notating each part as you sing.

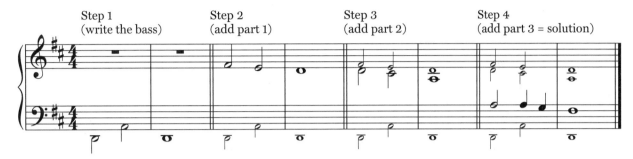

(2) In E minor, realize the progression i–V$^{8-7}$–i in four voices, SATB.

Sing the progression's melody, adjusting your syllables/numbers to those of minor. Notate each part as you sing.

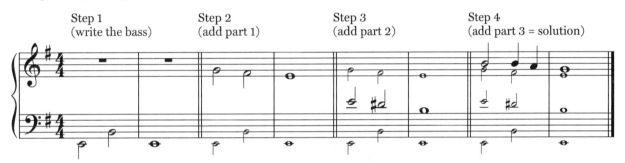

Note that the parts are realized in different voices in (1) and (2). Following this holistic approach will speed your work and make it more consistent. To avoid errors, just be mindful of these fundamental concepts.

- Match syllables/numbers to letter names and staff position accurately. For example, in E minor, *fa* ($\hat{4}$) is A; and in any minor key, *ti* ($\hat{7}$) requires an accidental.
- Keep each voice within its proper range. Keep the spacing one octave or less between the soprano and alto voices, and between the alto and tenor.

B. The cadential $^6_4$: V$^{6-5}_{4-3}$

The cadential $^6_4$ is a melodic embellishment of V. Strong-beat pitches *mi* ($\hat{3}$) and *do* ($\hat{1}$) delay the weak beat resolution of chord tones *re* ($\hat{2}$) and *ti* ($\hat{7}$); over bass pitch *sol* ($\hat{5}$), the melody *mi–re* ($\hat{3}$–$\hat{2}$) is represented by 6–5, while melody *do–ti* ($\hat{1}$–$\hat{7}$) is represented by 4–3. Compare the voice-leading below with that of exercise A: the parts are identical.

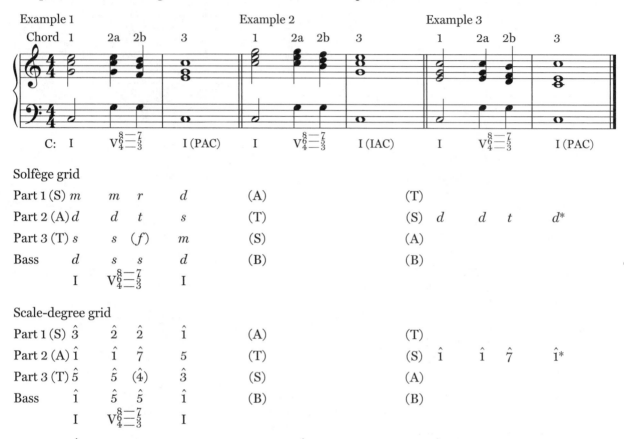

Solfège grid

Part 1 (S)	*m*	*m*	*r*	*d*	(A)		(T)				
Part 2 (A)	*d*	*d*	*t*	*s*	(T)		(S)	*d*	*d*	*t*	*d**
Part 3 (T)	*s*	*s*	(*f*)	*m*	(S)		(A)				
Bass	*d*	*s*	*s*	*d*	(B)		(B)				
	I	V$^{8-7}_{4-3}$		I							

Scale-degree grid

Part 1 (S)	$\hat{3}$	$\hat{2}$	$\hat{2}$	$\hat{1}$	(A)		(T)				
Part 2 (A)	$\hat{1}$	$\hat{1}$	$\hat{7}$	5	(T)		(S)	$\hat{1}$	$\hat{1}$	$\hat{7}$	$\hat{1}$*
Part 3 (T)	$\hat{5}$	$\hat{5}$	($\hat{4}$)	$\hat{3}$	(S)		(A)				
Bass	$\hat{1}$	$\hat{5}$	$\hat{5}$	$\hat{1}$	(B)		(B)				
	I	V$^{8-7}_{4-3}$		I							

*When *ti* ($\hat{7}$) is in an outer voice, it must rise to *do* ($\hat{1}$). In an inner voice, *ti* ($\hat{7}$) may fall to *sol* ($\hat{5}$).

Focus on the bass pitch: (1) When you hear *do* ($\hat{1}$) in the bass, write I (or i). (2) When you hear *sol* ($\hat{5}$) in the bass, write V. Did you hear *fa* ($\hat{4}$) above it? Write V⁷. (3) When you hear *sol–sol* ($\hat{5}$–$\hat{5}$) in the bass, write $V^6_4 {-} ^5_3$. Did you hear *fa* ($\hat{4}$) above it? Write $V^{8-7}_{4} {-}^{}_{3}$. To confirm that you heard the cadential $^6_4$, listen for melody *mi–re* or *do–ti* ($\hat{3}$–$\hat{2}$ or $\hat{1}$–$\hat{7}$).

Memorize the cadential $^6_4$ separately. Because its figures descend in order, 8–7–6–5–4–3, sing first the bass part, then parts 3 (8–7), 1 (6–5), and 2 (4–3). Spelling the cadential $^6_4$ will be as easy as finding the dominant pitch and singing down the scale from it.

The cadential $^6_4$ sung as melody

Now notate the cadential $^6_4$ in four voices, SATB, E♭ major.

Sing the progression's melody, notating each part as you sing.

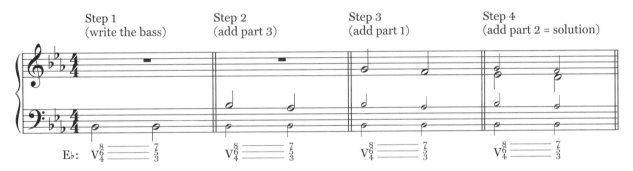

Lesson 9: Adding Predominant Chords to the Basic Phrase

Learn the models below, then perform them in major and minor keys from three flats to three sharps.

A. IV and ii⁶

When they precede V, chords IV and ii⁶ function as predominant chords (PD).

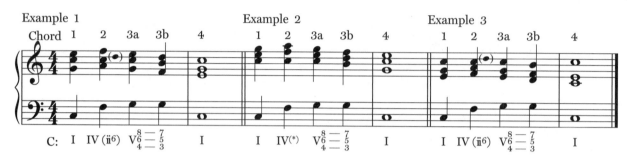

Solfège grid

Part 1 (S)	m	f	m	r		d	(A)				(T)
Part 2 (A)	d	$d(r)$	d	t		s	(T)	d	$d(*)$	d	t	s	(S)	d	$d(r)$	d	t	d^+
Part 3 (T)	s	l	s	f		m	(S)				(A)
Bass	d	f	s	s		d	(B)				(B)

I IV (ii⁶) $V_{4\ -\ 3}^{8\ -\ 7}$ I

Scale-degree grid

Part 1 (S)	$\hat{3}$	$\hat{4}$	$\hat{3}$	$\hat{2}$		$\hat{1}$	(A)				(T)
Part 2 (A)	$\hat{1}$	$\hat{1}(\hat{2})$	$\hat{1}$	$\hat{7}$		$\hat{5}$	(T)	$\hat{1}$	$\hat{1}(*)$	$\hat{1}$	$\hat{7}$	$\hat{5}$	(S)	$\hat{1}$	$\hat{1}(\hat{2})$	$\hat{1}$	$\hat{7}$	$\hat{1}^+$
Part 3 (T)	$\hat{5}$	$\hat{6}$	$\hat{5}$	$\hat{4}$		$\hat{3}$	(S)				(A)
Bass	$\hat{1}$	$\hat{4}$	$\hat{5}$	$\hat{5}$		$\hat{1}$	(B)				(B)

I IV (ii⁶) $V_{4\ -\ 3}^{8\ -\ 7}$ I

*Chord ii⁶ cannot harmonize this soprano because it would create parallel fifths.
⁺When *ti* ($\hat{7}$) is in an outer voice, it must rise to *do* ($\hat{1}$).

GETTING THE MOST OUT OF THIS LESSON

- To perform ii⁶, substitute the parenthetical pitch, *re* ($\hat{2}$), for *do* ($\hat{1}$) in part 2.
- In ii⁶, always keep *re* ($\hat{2}$) over *la* ($\hat{6}$) to avoid parallel fifths between I and ii⁶. See examples 1 and 3.

- To perform the progression I–IV(ii⁶)–V–I, omit chord 3a.
- To omit the seventh from V, repeat *sol* ($\hat{5}$) in chord 3b in part 3.
- To create a half cadence, omit chord 4.
- To prolong I with IV, play chords 1–2–1.

Memorize this and every new progression's voice-leading by singing its lines as a melody. Recalling the melody will help you accurately perform, write, and analyze common progressions. Refer to Lesson 8 to recall how to do this.

Strategies for hearing IV and ii⁶: In the bass, you hear *fa* ($\hat{4}$) rise to *sol* ($\hat{5}$). *Sol* ($\hat{5}$) supports V, but which chord harmonizes *fa* ($\hat{4}$)? Memorize these strategies; recalling even one of them will help you distinguish these chords.

	Major key			Minor key		
Chord quality	major	minor		minor	diminished	
Melodic pitch	*do* ($\hat{1}$)	*re* ($\hat{2}$)		*do* ($\hat{1}$)	*re* ($\hat{2}$)	
Common tone with tonic?	yes, *do* ($\hat{1}$)	no		yes, *do* ($\hat{1}$)	no	
Common tone with V?	no	yes, *re* ($\hat{2}$)		no	yes, *re* ($\hat{2}$)	
Tritone?	no	no		no	yes	
The chord is:	IV	ii⁶	V	iv	ii°⁶	V
Bass line:	*fa* ($\hat{4}$) ⟶		*sol* ($\hat{5}$)	*fa* ($\hat{4}$) ⟶		*sol* ($\hat{5}$)

B. The Neapolitan sixth chord: N⁶

The voice-leading for the N⁶ chord is identical to that for the ii⁶ chord; just substitute *ra* ($\flat\hat{2}$) for *re* ($\hat{2}$). Perform exercise A's examples 1 and 3 again, which are realized in C minor below.

Example 1   Example 3

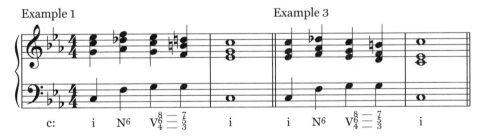

c: i   N⁶   V$^{8-7}_{6-5}_{4-3}$ i   i   N⁶   V$^{8-7}_{6-5}_{4-3}$ i

Over a *fa–sol* ($\hat{4}$–$\hat{5}$) bass line, if *fa* ($\hat{4}$) supports a chromatic chord, you hear the N⁶.

Lesson 10: Dominant-Function Seventh Chords

Learn the models below, then perform them in major and minor keys from three flats to three sharps. For the inversions of V⁷, perform chords 1, 2a, and 3. For vii⁷, play chords 1, 2b, and 3.

A. The V⁷ chord in inversion

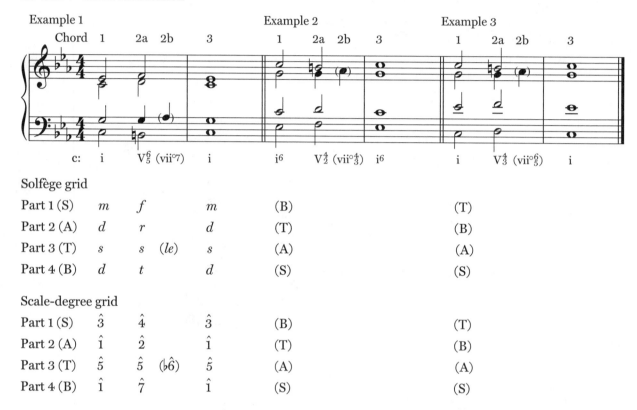

Solfège grid

Part 1 (S)	*m*	*f*		*m*	(B)		(T)	
Part 2 (A)	*d*	*r*		*d*	(T)		(B)	
Part 3 (T)	*s*	*s*	(*le*)	*s*	(A)		(A)	
Part 4 (B)	*d*	*t*		*d*	(S)		(S)	

Scale-degree grid

Part 1 (S)	$\hat{3}$	$\hat{4}$		$\hat{3}$	(B)		(T)	
Part 2 (A)	$\hat{1}$	$\hat{2}$		$\hat{1}$	(T)		(B)	
Part 3 (T)	$\hat{5}$	$\hat{5}$	($\flat\hat{6}$)	$\hat{5}$	(A)		(A)	
Part 4 (B)	$\hat{1}$	$\hat{7}$		$\hat{1}$	(S)		(S)	

The specific inversion of the dominant-function chord determines which part must appear in the bass. For example, if the dominant-function chord is V⁶₅, part 4 must appear in the bass because it contains *ti* ($\hat{7}$), the required bass pitch of V⁶₅.

V⁷ chord	vii°⁷ chord	Required bass pitch	Part # of bass
V⁶₅	vii°⁷	*ti* ($\hat{7}$)	4
V⁴₃	vii°⁶₅	*re* ($\hat{2}$)	2
V⁴₂	vii°⁴₃	*fa* ($\hat{4}$)	1

The vii⁴₂ chord does not occur very often, but when it does, it precedes the cadential ⁶₄. Again, memorize this voice-leading by singing its lines as a melody.

B. The vii⁷ chord and its inversions

Like V, the leading-tone seventh chord is a dominant-function chord. When preceding the tonic with vii⁷, vii⁴₃, or vii⁶₅, parts 1, 2, and 4 of exercise A remain identical to those of V⁷. In part 3, substitute parenthetical pitch *le* ($\flat\hat{6}$) for *sol* ($\hat{5}$).

Lesson 11: More Dominant–Tonic (D–T) Progressions

Learn the models below, then perform them in major and minor keys from three flats to three sharps.

A. *D–r–m* bass line with passing-chord harmonizations

In a *do–re–me* ($\hat{1}$–$\hat{2}$–$\flat\hat{3}$) bass line, *do* ($\hat{1}$) and *me* ($\flat\hat{3}$) are harmonized with I and I⁶, respectively. Between them is one of four possible dominant-function chords: V_3^4, $vii^{\circ6}_5$, V_4^6, or $vii^{\circ6}$.

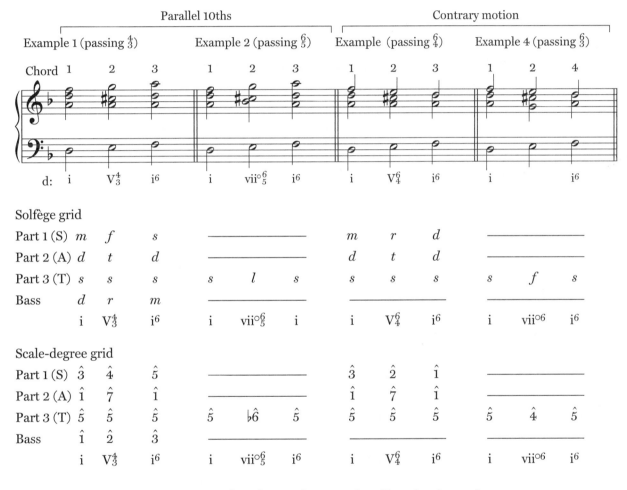

D–r–m bass line listening strategies: If you hear a *do–re–me* bass line, chords 1 and 3 are i and i⁶. Which passing chord is chord 2?

Do you hear parallel 10ths?		Or contrary motion?	
/	\	/	\
a common tone with i?	no common tone with i?	a common tone with i?	no common tone with i?
sol ($\hat{5}$)?	*le* ($\flat\hat{6}$)?	*sol* ($\hat{5}$)?	*fa* ($\hat{4}$)?
a Mm7 chord?	a dd7 chord?	a major triad?	a diminished triad?
1 tritone?	2 tritones?	no tritone?	1 tritone?
i V_3^4 i⁶	i $vii^{\circ6}_5$ i⁶	i V_4^6 i⁶	i $vii^{\circ6}$ i⁶

B. Summary of strategies for hearing dominant-tonic progressions

Listen to the voice-leading:

- $V^{(7)}$ contains *ti* ($\hat{7}$), which in an outer voice must lead to *do* ($\hat{1}$) in the tonic chord.
- V^7 contains *fa* ($\hat{4}$), which usually falls toward *mi* ($\hat{3}$) in the tonic chord.
- *Sol* ($\hat{5}$) is a common tone between I and V, and is often retained in the same voice.

Listen for common dominant-function-to-tonic (D–T) bass lines:

Bass line	Probable progression
sol–do ($\hat{5}$–$\hat{1}$)	Write V–I. If you hear *fa* ($\hat{4}$) in chord 1, write V^7–I.
sol–sol–do ($\hat{5}$–$\hat{5}$–$\hat{1}$)	Write V^{6-5}_{4-3}–I. If you hear *fa* ($\hat{4}$), write $V^{\substack{8-7\\6\\4-3}}$.
ti–do ($\hat{7}$–$\hat{1}$)	Default response: Write V^6–I. If you hear *fa* ($\hat{4}$) in chord 1, write V^6_5–I. (In minor: In chord 1, if you hear *le* ($\flat\hat{6}$) or a diminished quality, write vii°7.)
fa–mi ($\hat{4}$–$\hat{3}$)	If you hear *ti* ($\hat{7}$) in chord 1, write V^4_2–I^6. (In minor: In chord 1, if you hear *le* ($\flat\hat{6}$) or a diminished quality, write vii°$^4_3$.)
do–re–mi ($\hat{1}$–$\hat{2}$–$\hat{3}$)	Chords 1 and 3 are I and I^6. Determine the harmonization of *re* ($\hat{2}$), chord 2.

Over *d–r–m*, which motion occurs?

(1) Parallel 10ths (*mi–fa–sol*; $\hat{3}$–$\hat{4}$–$\hat{5}$):   Chord 2 is V^4_3 or vii°$^6_5$. Apply the *d–r–m* bass line listening strategies above.

(2) Contrary motion (*mi–re–do*; $\hat{3}$–$\hat{2}$–$\hat{1}$):   Chord 2 is V^6_4 or vii°^{6}. Apply the *d–r–m* bass line listening strategies above.

Lesson 12: Predominant Expansion of the Tonic

Each part of this lesson demonstrates common ways in which predominant chords may prolong the tonic. Once you have memorized these model progressions, transpose them to major and minor keys from three flats to three sharps.

A. The neighboring (pedal) $^6_4$ chord

The neighboring $^6_4$ chord is a melodic embellishment of a root-position major or minor triad, often the tonic chord. The chord is prolonged by means of upper neighbor tones in the voices that include the chord's third and fifth.

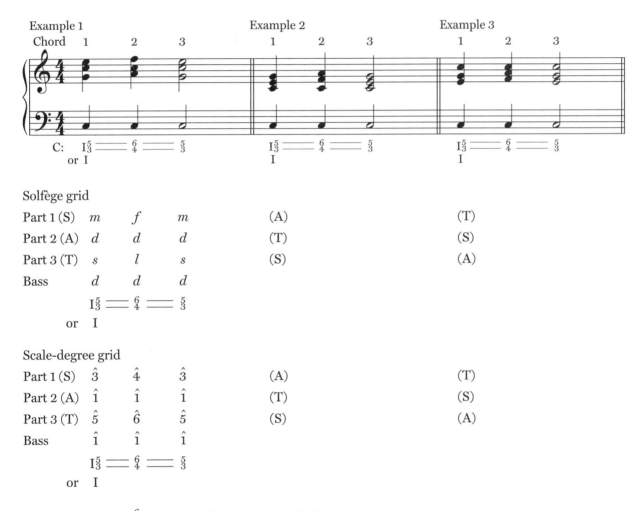

Solfège grid

Part 1 (S)	m	f	m	(A)			(T)	
Part 2 (A)	d	d	d	(T)			(S)	
Part 3 (T)	s	l	s	(S)			(A)	
Bass	d	d	d					

$$\text{I}^5_3 = {}^6_4 = {}^5_3$$
or I

Scale-degree grid

Part 1 (S)	$\hat{3}$	$\hat{4}$	$\hat{3}$	(A)			(T)	
Part 2 (A)	$\hat{1}$	$\hat{1}$	$\hat{1}$	(T)			(S)	
Part 3 (T)	$\hat{5}$	$\hat{6}$	$\hat{5}$	(S)			(A)	
Bass	$\hat{1}$	$\hat{1}$	$\hat{1}$					

$$\text{I}^5_3 = {}^6_4 = {}^5_3$$
or I

NEIGHBORING $^6_4$ LISTENING STRATEGIES

- The chord's root is sustained or repeated.
- The bass is often the tonic, subdominant, or dominant pitch. The most common, the tonic, is shown above.
- In any neighboring $^6_4$, the chord's third and fifth are embellished with upper neighbor tones. With the I chord, this creates melodies *mi–fa–mi* and *sol–la–sol* ($\hat{3}$–$\hat{4}$–$\hat{3}$; $\hat{5}$–$\hat{6}$–$\hat{5}$).

B. I–IV–I and I–IV–I⁶

The IV chord is often used to prolong the tonic. For I–IV–I, perform chords 1–2–1. For I–IV–I⁶ perform chords 1–2–3.

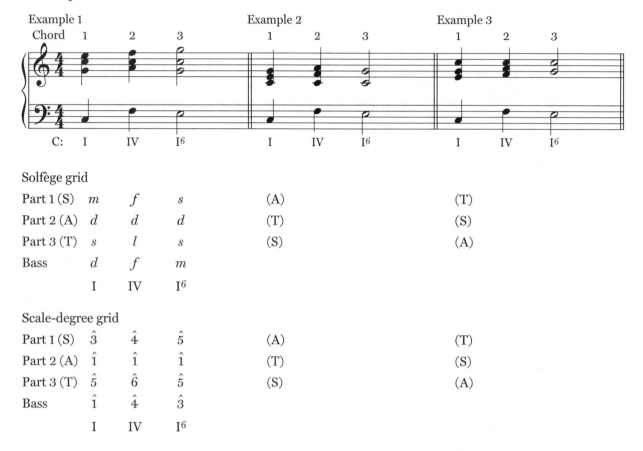

Solfège grid

Part 1 (S)	m	f	s	(A)			(T)		
Part 2 (A)	d	d	d	(T)			(S)		
Part 3 (T)	s	l	s	(S)			(A)		
Bass	d	f	m						
	I	IV	I⁶						

Scale-degree grid

Part 1 (S)	$\hat{3}$	$\hat{4}$	$\hat{5}$	(A)			(T)		
Part 2 (A)	$\hat{1}$	$\hat{1}$	$\hat{1}$	(T)			(S)		
Part 3 (T)	$\hat{5}$	$\hat{6}$	$\hat{5}$	(S)			(A)		
Bass	$\hat{1}$	$\hat{4}$	$\hat{3}$						
	I	IV	I⁶						

Listening strategies: In either progression, the tonic chord's fifth is embellished with its upper neighbor tone, *sol–la–sol* ($\hat{5}$–$\hat{6}$–$\hat{5}$). In I–IV–I, the tonic chord's third and fifth are embellished with upper neighbor tones. Compared with V$^4_2$–I⁶, there is no leading tone above the *fa–mi* ($\hat{4}$–$\hat{3}$) bass. I–IV–I⁶ often features a *mi–fa–sol* ($\hat{3}$–$\hat{4}$–$\hat{5}$) melodic line.

C. Skipping down from *do* ($\hat{1}$): Bass lines *d–l–f* ($\hat{1}$–$\hat{6}$–$\hat{4}$) and *d–l–m* ($\hat{1}$–$\hat{6}$–$\hat{3}$)

(1) *D–l–f* bass line: i–VI–PD–V$^{8-7}_{6-3}_{4-3}$–i

Compared with Lesson 9 A, chord 2 has been inserted, which creates a falling arpeggio, *d–l–f* ($\hat{1}$–$\hat{6}$–$\hat{4}$). Bass pitch *l* ($\hat{6}$) is typically harmonized with the submediant chord. Bass pitch *fa* ($\hat{4}$) is predominant (PD), and may be harmonized with iv, ii°6, ii°$^6_3$, or N6. Review the strategies in Lesson 9 to help you aurally distinguish these predominant chords.

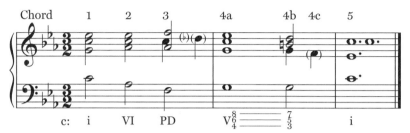

Solfège grid

Part 1 (S)	*m*	*m*	*f*		*m*	*r*	*d*
Part 2 (A)	*d*	*d*	*d*	(*r*)	*d*	*t*	*d**
Part 3 (T)	*s*	*l*	*l*		*s*	*s* (*f*)	*m*
Bass	*d*	*l*	*f*		*s*	*s*	*d*
	I	VI	PD		V$^8_6_4$ ═══	$^7_3$	i

Scale-degree grid

Part 1 (S)	$\hat{3}$	$\hat{3}$	$\hat{4}$		$\hat{3}$	$\hat{2}$	$\hat{1}$
Part 2 (A)	$\hat{1}$	$\hat{1}$	$\hat{1}$	($\hat{2}$)	$\hat{1}$	$\hat{7}$	$\hat{1}$*
Part 3 (T)	$\hat{5}$	$\hat{6}$	$\hat{6}$		$\hat{5}$	$\hat{5}$ ($\hat{4}$)	$\hat{3}$
Bass	$\hat{1}$	$\hat{6}$	$\hat{4}$		$\hat{5}$	$\hat{5}$	$\hat{1}$
	I	VI	PD		V$^8_6_4$ ═══	$^7_3$	i

* Take *ti* ($\hat{7}$) to *do* ($\hat{1}$) when in the soprano voice. In an inner voice, *ti* ($\hat{7}$) may fall to *sol* ($\hat{5}$).

The chart below shows which pitch(es) belong to the predominant chord (PD). This pitch will appear in part 2.

Predominant chord 3	Include pitch(es)	Exclude pitch
iv	*do* ($\hat{1}$)	*re* ($\hat{2}$)
ii°6	*re* ($\hat{2}$)	*do* ($\hat{1}$)
N6	*ra* ($\flat\hat{2}$), the parenthetical flat	*do* ($\hat{1}$)
ii°$^6_5$	*do* ($\hat{1}$) and *re* ($\hat{2}$)	*fa* ($\hat{4}$) from part 1

To play V instead of the cadential $^6_4$, skip from chord 3 to 4b. At 4c, don't play parenthetical pitch *fa* ($\hat{4}$). To play V7 instead of the cadential $^6_4$, skip from chord 3 to 4b; at 4c, play parenthetical pitch *fa* ($\hat{4}$).

GENERAL GUIDELINES

- For a half cadence, conclude with chord 4b.

- In minor keys, remember to include the leading tone in the dominant chord.

- To perform the progression in the parallel major, change the key signature and adjust the chord symbols to those of major keys: I–vi–IV (ii⁶ or ii$^6_5$)–V$^{8-7}_{6-5}_{4-3}$–I. The voice-leading and grids are identical, as are the pitches that distinguish one predominant chord from another.

- When using ii⁶ in major keys, always keep part 2 over part 3 to avoid parallel fifths leading into V$^{8-7}_{6-5}_{4-3}$.

(2) *D–l–m* bass line: I–IV⁶–I⁶

Chord 2 in exercise C (1) is replaced here by chords 2–3; the voice-leading is otherwise identical. These grids thus emphasize only the new progression.

Solfège grid

Part 1 (S)	*m*	*f*	*s*
Part 2 (A)	*d*	*d*	*d*
Part 3 (T)	*s*	*d*	*s*
Bass	*d*	*l*	*m*
	I	IV⁶	I⁶

Scale-degree grid

Part 1 (S)	$\hat{3}$	$\hat{4}$	$\hat{5}$
Part 2 (A)	$\hat{1}$	$\hat{1}$	$\hat{1}$
Part 3 (T)	$\hat{5}$	$\hat{1}$	$\hat{5}$
Bass	$\hat{1}$	$\hat{6}$	$\hat{3}$
	I	IV⁶	I⁶

LISTENING STRATEGIES FOR I–IV⁶–I⁶

- Listen for a *mi–fa–sol* ($\hat{3}$–$\hat{4}$–$\hat{5}$) soprano over a *do–la–mi* ($\hat{1}$–$\hat{6}$–$\hat{3}$) bass.

- *Do* ($\hat{1}$) is a common tone throughout the progression.

- In major keys, the triad qualities will all be major; in minor keys, they will all be minor.

- Compare this progression with that of exercise C (1).

D. The plagal resolution/cadence

In the PAC below, the final tonic chord is prolonged by means of a plagal resolution (chords 5–6). Occasionally a phrase concludes with the progression IV–I, in which case it is called a plagal cadence.

In the example below, chords 1–4 are identical to those of Lesson 9 A, example 1. Chords 4–6 incorporate the voice-leading from Lesson 12 A, example 3. Review the voice-leading grids and strategies found in those lessons.

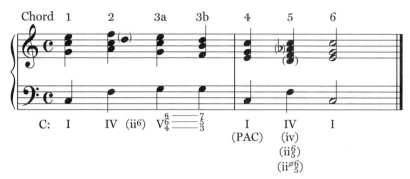

Varying chord 5: to play IV, exclude parenthetical pitch *re* ($\hat{2}$) and the parenthetical flat; to play iv, exclude parenthetical pitch *re* ($\hat{2}$); to play ii$_5^6$, include *re* ($\hat{2}$) and omit *la* ($\hat{6}$)/*le* ($\flat\hat{6}$); to play ii$^{\varnothing_5^6}$, exclude *fa* ($\hat{4}$), but include all parenthetical pitches.

Lesson 13: Deceptive and Phrygian Resolutions

Chapter 15 introduces deceptive and Phrygian resolutions, which appear in this lesson in exercises A and B. Chromatic Phrygian resolutions (augmented-sixth chords), introduced in Chapter 26, appear in exercise C. Memorize the model progressions, then transpose them to keys from three flats to three sharps.

A. The deceptive resolution/cadence

Example 1:
Authentic cadence with tripled root in I
Compare with Lesson 8 A and B, example 3.

Example 2:
Deceptive resolution/cadence
La ($\hat{6}$) replaces *do* ($\hat{1}$) in bass.
All upper voices remain the same.

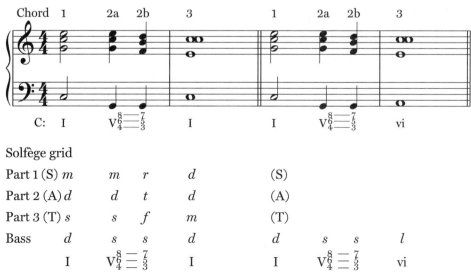

Solfège grid

Part 1 (S) *m*		*m*	*r*	*d*	(S)			
Part 2 (A) *d*		*d*	*t*	*d*	(A)			
Part 3 (T) *s*		*s*	*f*	*m*	(T)			
Bass *d*		*s*	*s*	*d*	*d*	*s*	*s*	*l*
I		V$_4^8$ — $_3^7$		I	I	V$_4^8$ — $_3^7$		vi

Scale-degree grid

Part 1 (S)	$\hat{3}$	$\hat{3}$	$\hat{2}$	$\hat{1}$	(S)			
Part 2 (A)	$\hat{1}$	$\hat{1}$	$\hat{7}$	$\hat{1}$	(A)			
Part 3 (T)	$\hat{5}$	$\hat{5}$	$\hat{4}$	$\hat{3}$	(T)			
Bass	$\hat{1}$	$\hat{5}$	$\hat{5}$	$\hat{1}$	$\hat{1}$	$\hat{5}$	$\hat{5}$	$\hat{6}$
	I	V^{8-7}_{4-3}		I	I	V^{8-7}_{4-3}		vi

Variations: Switch between authentic and deceptive resolutions; only the bass pitch changes. For V7–vi, omit chord 2a in example 2. For V–vi, omit chord 2a and substitute *sol* ($\hat{5}$) for *fa* ($\hat{4}$) in chord 2b. Review Lesson 12 C; in the final chord of (1) and (2), change the bass pitch to create a deceptive cadence.

Listen for:

- *sol–la* ($\hat{5}$–$\hat{6}$) or *sol–le* ($\hat{5}$–$\flat\hat{6}$) in the bass;
- rising parallel 10ths over the *sol–la* ($\hat{5}$–$\hat{6}$) or *sol–le* ($\hat{5}$–$\flat\hat{6}$) bass;
- *ti–do* ($\hat{7}$–$\hat{1}$) in an upper part;
- contrary motion against the bass in the other two upper parts;
- *do* ($\hat{1}$) to be doubled, just as it would be if the chord were tonic.

B. Diatonic Phrygian resolution: The *le–sol* ($\flat\hat{6}$–$\hat{5}$) bass line

The Phrygian cadence occurs in minor keys as a special type of half cadence. Bass pitch *sol* ($\hat{5}$) is preceded by *le* ($\flat\hat{6}$) and harmonized with iv⁶–V. The bass line of chords 3–6 below typifies the approach to V—a descending tetrachord *do–te–le–sol* ($\hat{1}$–$\flat\hat{7}$–$\flat\hat{6}$–$\hat{5}$).

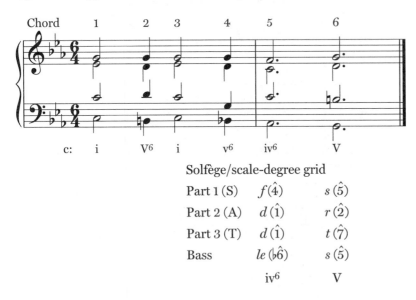

Solfège/scale-degree grid

Part 1 (S)	*f* ($\hat{4}$)	*s* ($\hat{5}$)
Part 2 (A)	*d* ($\hat{1}$)	*r* ($\hat{2}$)
Part 3 (T)	*d* ($\hat{1}$)	*t* ($\hat{7}$)
Bass	*le* ($\flat\hat{6}$)	*s* ($\hat{5}$)
	iv⁶	V

At the Phrygian cadence, *sol* ($\hat{5}$) is approached by step from below and above: listen for bass pitch *le* ($\flat\hat{6}$) to fall to *sol* ($\hat{5}$); listen in the upper voices for *fa* ($\hat{4}$) to rise to *sol* ($\hat{5}$). Listen for the bass descent *do–te–le–sol* ($\hat{1}$–$\flat\hat{7}$–$\flat\hat{6}$–$\hat{5}$). Since *do* ($\hat{1}$) is doubled in iv⁶, one must fall to *ti* ($\hat{7}$) while the other rises to *re* ($\hat{2}$).

C. Chromatic Phrygian resolution: Augmented-sixth chords (A⁶–V)

Example 1 includes a chromatic passing tone in m. 2's soprano voice: *fa–fi–sol* ($\hat{4}$-$\sharp\hat{4}$-$\hat{5}$). At chord 5b, the interval between bass and soprano is an augmented sixth, which is why the resultant chord is called an augmented-sixth chord (A⁶ chord). We can understand the A⁶ chord and its resolution as a chromaticized Phrygian resolution.

Example 1: Phrygian cadence embellished with a chromatic passing tone, *fi* ($\sharp\hat{4}$)

All three types of A⁶ chords share three pitches—*le* ($\flat\hat{6}$), *fi* ($\sharp\hat{4}$), and *do* ($\hat{1}$). The fourth pitch—*do* ($\hat{1}$), *re* ($\hat{2}$), or *me* ($\flat\hat{3}$)—determines whether the chord is Italian (It⁶), French (Fr⁶), or German (Gr⁶), respectively.

Example 2: Italian, French, and German augmented-sixth chords

Solfège grid

Part 1 (S)	*fi*			*s*
Part 2 (A)	*d*	*r*	*me*	*r*
Part 3 (T)	*d*			*t*
Bass	*le*			*s*
	It⁶	Fr⁶	Gr⁶	V

Scale-degree grid

Part 1 (S)	$\sharp\hat{4}$			$\hat{5}$
Part 2 (A)	$\hat{1}$	$\hat{2}$	$\flat\hat{3}$	$\hat{2}$
Part 3 (T)	$\hat{1}$			$\hat{7}$
Bass	$\flat\hat{6}$			$\hat{5}$
	It⁶	Fr⁶	Gr⁶	V

In a Phrygian resolution (diatonic or chromatic), bass pitch *le* ($\flat\hat{6}$) falls to *sol* ($\hat{5}$). *Sol* ($\hat{5}$) supports V, but which is the predominant chord? If the chord that harmonizes *le* ($\flat\hat{6}$) is diatonic, it's iv⁶. If the chord is chromatic, it's A⁶. If the chord is A⁶, determine its type:

It⁶	**Fr⁶**	**Gr⁶**
Do ($\hat{1}$) is doubled.	*Re* ($\hat{2}$)	*Me* ($\flat\hat{3}$)
Only three pitches.	M2, *do–re* ($\hat{1}$–$\hat{2}$).	Chord sounds like a dominant 7th chord.
	Common tone with V.	Parallel fifths into V.

Memorizing the melody below will help you recall the voice-leading for A⁶–V. The chart underneath shows how the melody relates to the chords and voice-leading.

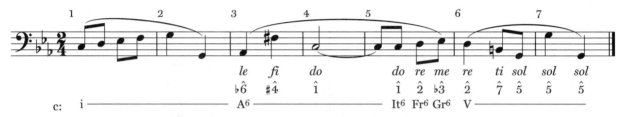

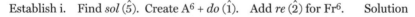

Measure(s)	Purpose
1–2	Establish the minor key.
2	Locates *sol* ($\hat{5}$), the dominant pitch.
3	Creates the A⁶ interval as chromatic upper and lower neighbor tones to *sol* ($\hat{5}$).
3–4	Contain the three pitches common to all A⁶ chords.
5	Contains the pitches that determine whether the A⁶ chord is It⁶, Fr⁶, or Gr⁶.
6–7	Contain the resolution to the V chord.

Now realize the progression Fr⁶–V in E minor in four parts, SATB.

Lesson 14: Delayed Resolutions

The voice-leading in this lesson is identical to that of Lessons 8 A and 10 A. Review the earlier lessons before completing this one.

Delaying the resolution of a part may create a strong-beat dissonance called a **suspension** or **retardation**. Suspensions resolve down, and retardations resolve up. Delayed resolutions are indicated in the figured bass as a dissonance (nonchord tone) followed by its consonant resolution (chord tone); e.g., 9–8, 7–8, 7–6, 4–3, 2–3.

A. Incorporating delayed resolutions into Lesson 8 A

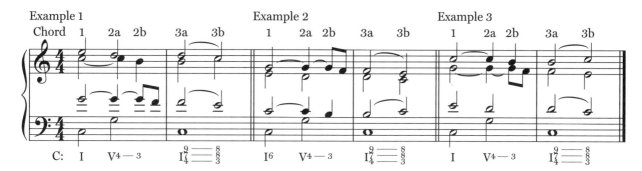

B. Incorporating delayed resolutions into Lesson 10 A

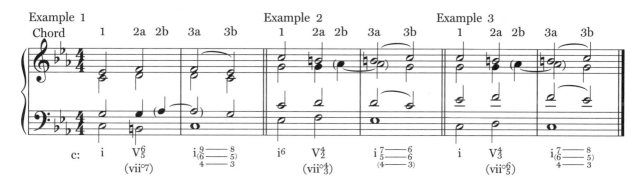

VARIATIONS

- In the first measure of example 1, make bass pitch *do* ($\hat{1}$) a dotted-half note and *ti* ($\hat{7}$) a quarter note. This creates a 2–3 bass suspension at chord 2a, which resolves at 2b.
- In each example, substitute parenthetical pitch *le* ($\flat\hat{6}$) for *sol* ($\hat{5}$), sustain it over the change of bass at chord 3a, and resolve down by step at 3b. In examples 1 and 3, this creates a 6–5 resolution (the "consonant" suspension), and in example 2 a 4–3 suspension.

Lesson 15: Sequences

Common sequences include descending fifths, descending thirds, descending $^6_3$ chords, and ascending 5–6. Diatonic models of each sequence appear first, followed by their chromatic variants.

A linear intervallic pattern (LIP) is the recurring harmonic interval pattern between the outer voices. When part 2 or 3 appears as the soprano, calculate and name the new LIP.

Memorize each model in its original key, then transpose it to keys ranging from three flats to three sharps. In a minor key, the descending-fifth progression is i–iv–VII–III–VI–ii°–V–i, and the descending-third is i–v–VI–III–iv–ii⌀7–V7–i.

A. Descending fifths

(1) Diatonic descending fifths (Chapter 19)

For all diatonic descending-fifth sequences, the upper three parts may be realized in any voice.

(a) Successive root-position triads

(b) Alternating root-position and first-inversion triads

(c) Successive seventh chords

Successive seventh chords produce a characteristic LIP between two parts and the bass. Play the example to hear how the soprano moves 10–7 against the bass while the tenor simultaneously moves 7–10. Omit the alto to play a common three-voice variant of this sequence.

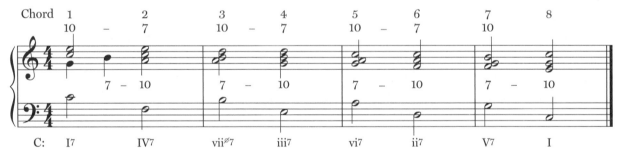

(2) Chromatic descending fifths (Chapters 20ff.)

When performing any of the chromatic descending-fifth models:

- *To review the diatonic progression*, play none of the parenthetical pitches. The analysis of the diatonic progression appears immediately beneath the staff.

- *To tonicize a chord*, play the parenthetical pitch(es) in the chord before it. For example, to tonicize vi (chord 5), play the parenthetical pitch in chord 4.

- *To create a secondary dominant*, play a chord's parenthetical pitch(es). The chromatic chord's analysis appears in parentheses beneath the staff.

- *To modulate*, choose the destination key; play from the beginning with diatonic pitches; and, in the chord before the destination, include the parenthetical pitch(es). For example, to modulate to the dominant (chord 7), add the accidental to chord 6; to modulate to the relative minor (chord 5), add the accidental to chord 4.

(a) Successive root-position triads

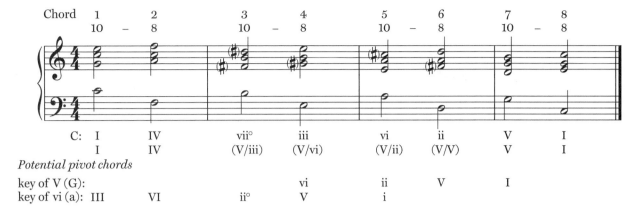

Potential pivot chords

key of V (G):
key of vi (a):

(b) Alternating root-position and first-inversion chords

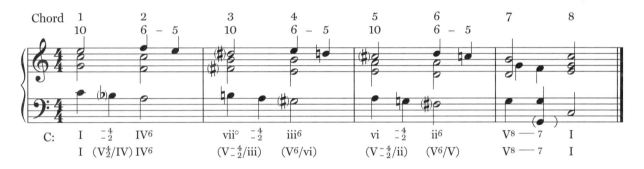

(c) Successive seventh chords

In this sequence, you often hear only the soprano, tenor, and bass. Practice this three-voice version, too.

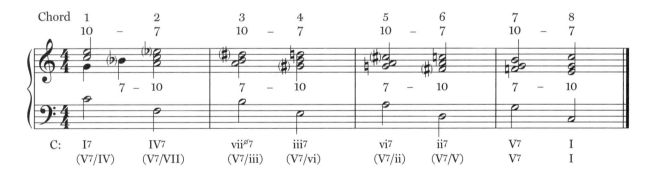

B. Descending thirds

In both diatonic and chromatic progressions, the bass and alto of model (a) switch parts in model (c). In (a) and (b), the soprano and alto make characteristic soprano voices. Model (c) appears most often with the given soprano.

(1) Diatonic descending thirds (Chapter 19)

(a) Root-position chords with a 10–5 LIP

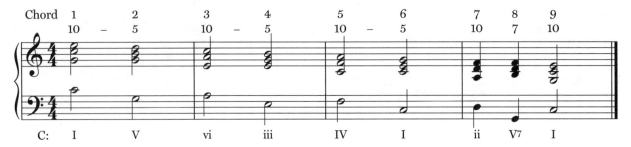

(b) Root-position chords with suspensions

(c) Alternating $\frac{5}{3}$ and $\frac{6}{3}$ triads with a 10–10 LIP

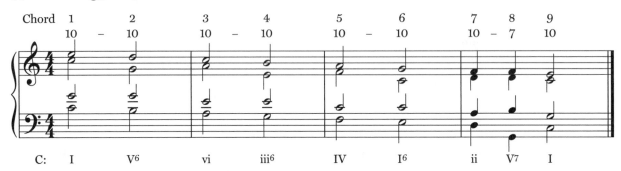

(2) Chromatic descending thirds (Chapters 20ff.)

The chromatic descending-third sequence is characteristic only in major keys.

(a) Alternating $\frac{5}{3}$ and $\frac{4}{3}$ with a 10–5 LIP

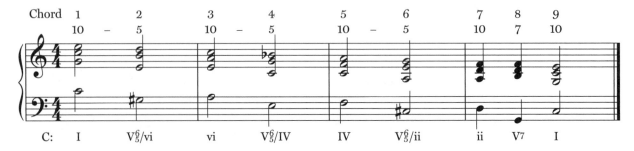

(b) Alternating $\frac{5}{3}$ and $\frac{4}{3}$ with suspensions

C: I   V$\frac{6}{4}$—3/vi   vi^9—8   V$\frac{6}{4}$—3/IV   IV^9—8   V$\frac{6}{4}$—3/ii   ii^9—V^7 I$\frac{9}{4}$=$\frac{8}{3}$

(c) Alternating $\frac{5}{3}$ and $\frac{4}{3}$ with a 10–10 LIP

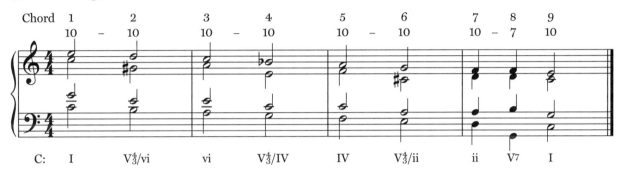

C: I   V$\frac{4}{3}$/vi   vi   V$\frac{4}{3}$/IV   IV   V$\frac{4}{3}$/ii   ii   V^7 I

C. Descending $\frac{6}{3}$ chords with 7–6 suspensions

Descending $\frac{6}{3}$ chords appear characteristically in only three voices.

(1) Major-key descending $\frac{6}{3}$ chords with 7–6 suspensions

(a) Diatonic (Chapter 19)

(b) Chromatic (Chapter 29)

(2) Minor-key descending $\frac{6}{3}$ chords with 7–6 suspensions

(a) Diatonic (Chapter 19)

(b) Chromatic (Chapter 29)

D. Ascending 5–6

(1) Diatonic ascending 5–6 (Chapter 19)

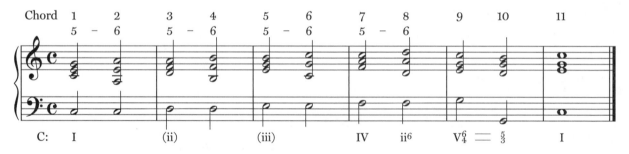

(2) Chromatic ascending 5–6 (Chapter 20)

The chromatic ascending 5–6 sequence is more common than the diatonic. It is the most common ascending sequence, and appears characteristically in major keys. The alto line makes a good soprano voice.

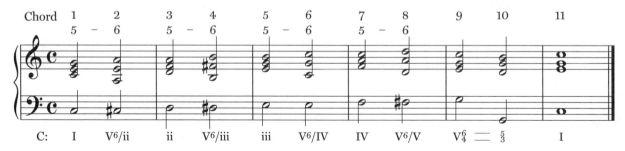

(3) Chromatic ascending 5–6 with a "reaching over" (Chapter 20)

In this common variant, the soprano skips up to the chordal seventh, which is called "reaching over," and the 5–6 appears in the tenor. The alto and tenor lines also make good soprano voices.

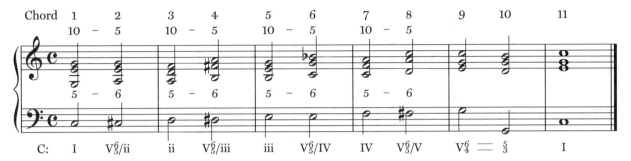

Lesson 16: Secondary-Dominant-Function Chords

The D–T voice-leading relationships you memorized in Lessons 8 and 10 can be applied to scale degrees other than the tonic. When this occurs, you hear a chromatic pitch that belongs to a secondary-dominant-function chord. Hearing how it resolves tells you which scale degree is tonicized.

A. Tonicizing V

(1) $V^{(7)}/V$

Perform each example below. In example 1, you hear V_5^6–I in G major. Example 2 sounds identical, but is in a new key—C major. In C major, G is the dominant; the bracket beneath the staff indicates that the chord progression above it functions in the key of the Roman numeral (V) below it.

Example 1: V_5^6–I in G major

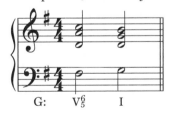

Example 2: V_5^6–I of V in C major

When you hear fi ($\sharp\hat{4}$), ask two questions: (1) Is fi ($\sharp\hat{4}$) a melodic embellishment, like a chromatic neighbor or passing tone? If so, there is no secondary dominant. (2) Is fi ($\sharp\hat{4}$) part of a chord that leads to V? If so, you probably hear a secondary dominant to V. ("Probably" because fi ($\sharp\hat{4}$) may imply another chromatic approach to V, the augmented-sixth chord.)

There are three ways to notate the secondary relationship: with a bracket, slash, or colon.

Bracket notation is excellent for aural analysis, good for written analysis.

   (a) Write D–T Roman numerals for the two chords.

   (b) Write a bracket under the chords to show you heard a secondary relationship.

   (c) Listen for the scale degree of the tonicized chord; beneath the bracket, write its Roman numeral.

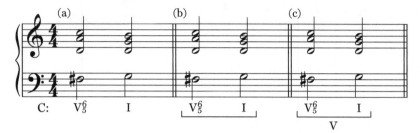

Slash notation is excellent for written analysis, good for aural analysis.

   (a) Write a slash to show the secondary relationship, followed by the Roman numeral of the tonicized chord.

   (b) Write the Roman numeral of the tonicized chord.

   (c) In the key of the tonicized chord and before the slash, write the chromatic chord's Roman numeral.

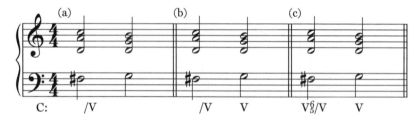

Colon notation is excellent for extended passages in a nontonic key, aural or written.

   (a) Write D–T Roman numerals for the two chords.

   (b) Before your D–T analysis, write the Roman numeral of the tonicized scale degree followed by a colon.

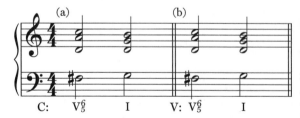

Before proceeding, review Lessons 8 A and 10 in their entirety. You will use their voice-leading and strategies to create progressions that tonicize V.

Example 1: Realize the progression below in four voices, SATB.

G: I   V8–7   I
          V

This is the progression you learned in Lesson 8 A. Follow its voice-leading and strategies.

- The V beneath the bracket indicates that *sol* ($\hat{5}$) is tonicized. In G major, *sol* ($\hat{5}$) is D.
- Thinking now in the key of D, perform the progression above the bracket: I–V$^{8-7}$–I.
- Sing the progression's melody in the key of D, notating each part as you sing. Since D major has two sharps, remember to perform an accidental on its leading tone, C♯.

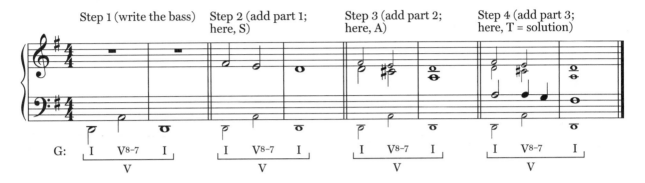

Example 2: Realize the progression below in four voices, SATB.

F: ⌐I   V$^6_5$ I⌐
          V

This is the first progression in Lesson 10 A. Follow its voice-leading and strategies.

- The V beneath the bracket indicates that *sol* ($\hat{5}$) is tonicized. In F major, *sol* ($\hat{5}$) is C.
- Thinking now in the key of C, perform the progression above the bracket: I–V$^6_5$–I.
- Sing the progression's melody in the key of C, notating each part as you sing. Since C major has no flats, remember to perform an accidental on its leading tone, B♮.

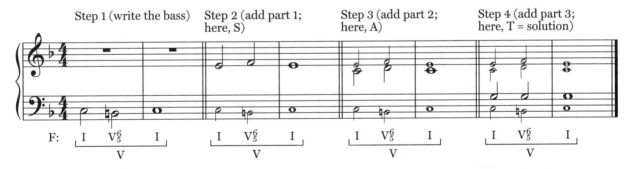

Now realize each progression below in four parts, SATB, in these keys: C, F, B♭, A, E♭, D.

Progression 1
⌐I   V$^{8-7}$ I⌐
          V

Progression 2
⌐I   V$^6_5$ I⌐
          V

Progression 3
⌐I   V$^4_2$ I⌐
          V

(2) vii7/V

Realize each progression below in four parts, SATB, in these keys: C, F, B♭, A, E♭, D.

Progression 1
⌐I   vii^{ø7} I⌐
          V

Progression 2
⌐I   vii$^{ø4}_3$ I⌐
          V

B. Tonicizing other scale degrees

Any scale degree on which a major or minor triad occurs may be tonicized.

Realize the progression below in four voices, SATB.

F: i   V$^6_5$ i
              vi

The vi beneath the bracket indicates that *la* ($\hat{6}$) is tonicized. In F major, *la* ($\hat{6}$) is D minor (vi). Thinking now in the key of D minor, perform the progression above the bracket: i–V$^6_5$–i. Sing the progression's melody in the key of D minor, notating each part as you sing. Remember to perform an accidental on its leading tone, C$\sharp$.

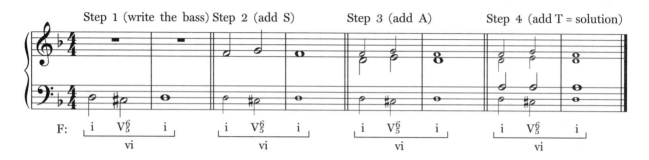

F: i V$^6_5$ i   i V$^6_5$ i   i V$^6_5$ i   i V$^6_5$ i
         vi   vi   vi   vi

(1) Now realize each progression below in four parts, SATB, in these keys: C, F, B$\flat$, A, E$\flat$, D.

Progression 1   Progression 2   Progression 3   Progression 4
  i   V$^6_5$ i   i   V$^6_5$ i   I^6 V$^4_2$ I^6 I^6 V$^4_2$ I^6
        vi   ii   IV   V

(2) *Secondary dominants in the chromatic ascending 5–6 sequence*: Perform Lesson 15 D (3). Chords 2–3, 4–5, 6–7, and 8–10 feature V$^6_5$–I progressions that tonicize a scale degree other than tonic. The voice-leading is identical to that from Lesson 10 A.

(3) *Secondary dominants in the chromatic descending-fifth sequence*: Review Lesson 15 B (1), (a), then perform Lesson 15 B (2), (a). Chromatic chords 3–4, 4–5, 5–6, and 6–7 feature V–I progressions that tonicize a scale degree other than tonic. The voice leading is identical to that from Lesson 8 A.

(4) *Secondary dominants in the chromatic descending-fifth sequence*: Review Lesson 15 A (1), (b), then perform Lesson 15 A (2), (b). Chromatic chords 1–2, 3–4, and 5–6 feature V$^4_2$–I^6 progressions, and chromatic chords 2–3, 4–5, and 6–8 feature V$^6_5$–I progressions. The voice-leading is identical to that from Lesson 10 A.

(5) Complete exercise (1) again, but for each form of V^7, substitute the corresponding form of vii^7 as shown below.

Progression 1   Progression 2   Progression 3   Progression 4
  i   vii^{o7} i   i   vii^{o7} i   I^6 vii$^{\varnothing4}_3$ I^6 I^6 vii$^{\varnothing4}_3$ I^6
        vi   ii   IV   V

(6) Complete exercises (2)–(4) again, but for each form of V^7, substitute the corresponding form of vii^7.

C. Secondary dominant–tonic (D–T) listening strategies

Hearing a chromatic pitch often signals a secondary D–T relationship. In this case, a chromatic pitch relates to the scale of the chord it tonicizes: a raised pitch sounds like *ti* ($\hat{7}$), while a lowered pitch sounds like *fa* ($\hat{4}$). The quality of the chord tonicized will be major or minor. Because it is easy to distinguish between these qualities, you can learn to quickly identify secondary dominants by ear.

(1) *Which chord is most likely?* Listen first for chord quality, then fine-tune your answer by identifying the chromatic pitch. In major keys, the most likely chord to be tonicized is V, followed by vi, IV, ii, and occasionally iii.

- If the quality of the tonicized chord is major, V is more likely than IV. (a) Did you hear *fi* (♯$\hat{4}$)? The chord is V. (b) Did you hear *te* (♭$\hat{7}$)? The chord is IV.
- If the quality of the tonicized chord is minor, vi is more likely than ii (outside of sequences, iii is seldom tonicized). (a) Did you hear *si* (♯$\hat{5}$)? The chord is vi. (b) Did you hear *di* (♯$\hat{1}$)? The chord is ii. (c) Did you hear *ri* (♯$\hat{2}$)? The chord is iii.

In minor keys, the most likely chord to be tonicized is III, the relative major. Also frequently tonicized are v and iv. Less common is VI, and VII is seldom tonicized.

- If the tonicized chord's quality is major, III and V are highly likely. Less likely is VI; VII is unlikely, but possible. (a) Did you hear *te* (♭$\hat{7}$) instead of *ti* ($\hat{7}$)? The chord is III. Since you expect *ti* ($\hat{7}$), *te* (♭$\hat{7}$) seems chromatic. (b) Did you hear *fi* (♯$\hat{4}$)? The chord is V. (c) Did you hear a deceptive resolution? The chord is VI. (d) Did you hear *la* ($\hat{6}$) move to *te* (♭$\hat{7}$)? The chord is VII.
- If the quality of the tonicized chord is minor, both v and iv are likely. (a) Did you hear *fi* (♯$\hat{4}$)? The chord is v. (In minor keys, the *chord* of V is major, but the *key* of v is minor.) (b) Did you hear *mi* ($\hat{3}$)? The chord is iv.

(2) Review the strategies for hearing dominant–tonic (D–T) progressions (Lesson 11 B). If the bass line is *ti–do* ($\hat{7}$–$\hat{1}$), write V⁶–I. If you hear *fa* ($\hat{4}$) in chord 1, write V⁷–I.

Imagine you hear the two-chord example below, in C major. Because F♯–G *sounds* like *ti–do* ($\hat{7}$–$\hat{1}$), at (a) write V$^6_5$–I beneath the staff. Since you hear a chromatic pitch, draw a bracket beneath the chord symbols at (b). Last, identify the chromatic pitch. Since *fi* (♯$\hat{4}$) tonicizes V, at (c) write V beneath the bracket to show this relationship.

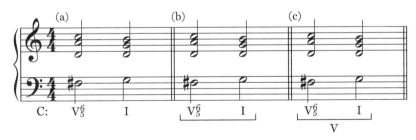

Lesson 17: Common Modulations (Chapters 22ff.)

To modulate, (1) establish the tonic key, (2) link the two keys, and (3) establish the destination key. From Lessons 9 A, 12 C (1), and 12 C (2) choose a progression to establish the tonic as well as the destination key.

Example 1: Modulate from I to V; I becomes IV in the key of V.

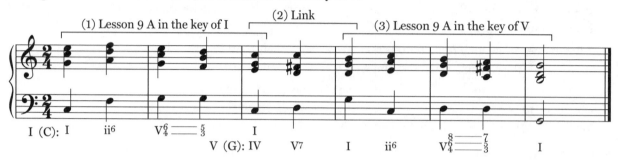

Example 2: Modulate from i to III; i becomes vi in the key of III.

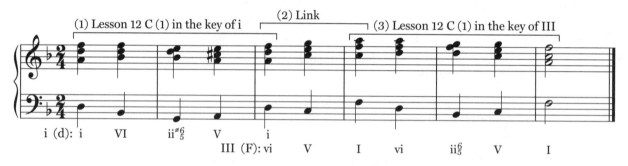

Now modulate from I to V or from i to III, beginning in each of the following tonic keys: F, G, D, C, and A.

Lesson 18: Modal Mixture (Chapters 25ff.)

Modal mixture typically occurs in major-key music when chords are borrowed from the parallel minor. Listen and look for modal scale degrees $\flat\hat{3}$, $\flat\hat{6}$, and $\flat\hat{7}$. In minor-key music, the most common form of mixture changes the quality of the final tonic from minor to major with a Picardy third; you expect to hear *me* ($\flat\hat{3}$), but instead hear *mi* ($\hat{3}$).

Each exercise below is a variation of a previous lesson. Because the voice-leading, grids, and strategies are conceptually identical to what you have already learned, you can add these borrowed chords to your tonal palette quickly and accurately.

A. Borrowed predominant chords

(1) Return to Lesson 9 A, and perform each progression. In chord 2, substitute *le* ($\flat\hat{6}$) for *la* ($\hat{6}$) to create borrowed chords iv or ii°6.

(2) Return to Lesson 12 A and B, and perform each progression. In chord 2, substitute *le* ($\flat\hat{6}$) for *la* ($\hat{6}$) to create a borrowed predominant chord.

(3) Return to Lesson 12 C (1), and perform it three different ways.

- Perform the entire progression in the parallel major key.
- Perform in the parallel major key again, but change chord 3 by substituting *le* (♭$\hat{6}$) for *la* ($\hat{6}$) to create borrowed chords iv, ii°⁶, or ii⌀⁶₅.
- Perform in the parallel major key, but change chord 2 to ♭VI by substituting *le* (♭$\hat{6}$) for *la* ($\hat{6}$) and *me* (♭$\hat{3}$) for *mi* ($\hat{3}$). Continue to substitute *le* (♭$\hat{6}$) for *la* ($\hat{6}$) in chord 3.

B. Borrowed leading-tone seventh chords

(1) Return to Lesson 10 B, and perform each progression in the parallel major. Substitute *le* (♭$\hat{6}$) for *la* ($\hat{6}$) to create different inversions of borrowed chord vii°7.

(2) Return to Lesson 11 A. Perform example 2 in the parallel major key, but substitute *le* (♭$\hat{6}$) for *la* ($\hat{6}$), thus including borrowed chord vii°⁶₅.

C. Borrowed tonic-function chords

(1) Return to Lesson 9 A. Perform each progression in the parallel minor key, but in chord 4, substitute *mi* ($\hat{3}$) for *me* (♭$\hat{3}$) (creating a Picardy third in borrowed chord I).

(2) Perform each progression in Lesson 9 A in the parallel minor key, but in chord 4's bass pitch, substitute *le* (♭$\hat{6}$) for *do* ($\hat{1}$) to create a deceptive cadence that features borrowed chord ♭VI.

(3) Return to Lesson 13 A. Perform example 2, but in chord 3's bass pitch, substitute *le* (♭$\hat{6}$) for *la* ($\hat{6}$) to create a deceptive cadence that features borrowed chord ♭VI.

Lesson 19: Blues and Popular-Music Harmony (Chapters 28ff.)

A. The blues

The blues scale is a minor-pentatonic scale plus a "flatted fifth" (e.g., in C, the F♯ or G♭). The scale's accidentals, called **blue notes**, are a form of modal mixture. Despite the accidentals, blues uses the major key signature of its tonic pitch.

C blues scale

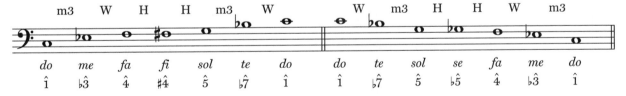

(1) Perform ascending and descending blues scales from B♭, F, E♭, D, A, D♭, G, and F♯. Sing with solfège syllables, scale-degree numbers, and letter names.

In its simplest harmonization, the blues progression features Mm7 chords on $\hat{1}$, $\hat{4}$, and $\hat{5}$. The slashes in the notation mean to keep time as you prolong and embellish each chord. Play first without the parenthetical chords (keep playing the previous chord), then with them to make a typical variant.

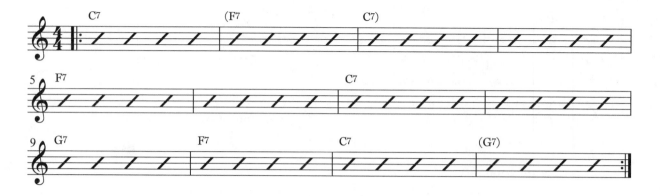

(2) Now play the blues progression, and sing motives from the blues scale in four-bar phrases. Transpose the progression to other keys and perform again.

B. Extensions in popular-music chords

To the popular-music symbols for triads and seventh chords you can add additional pitches called **extensions**. In popular music, extensions can be chord members, equal in importance to the root, third, fifth, and seventh.

Extensions to major or minor triads

Lead-sheet notations	What to play
Cmaj^6, Cma^6, CM^6, C^{add6}; C^{+6}, C$^{\triangle6}$, C^6	C major triad + M6
Cmin^6; Cmi^6, Cm^6, C^{-6}, c^{add6}	C minor triad + M6
Cmaj$^9_6$, Cma$^9_6$, CM$^9_6$, C$^{\triangle9}_6$, C$^9_6$	C major triad + M6 + M9
Cmin$^9_6$, Cmi$^9_6$, Cm$^9_6$, C$^{-9}_6$, c$^9_6$	C minor triad + M6 + M9
Csus^4, Csus	C, F, and G (the fourth displaces the third)

Extensions to seventh chords

Lead-sheet notations	What to play
Cmaj^9, Cma^9, CM^9, C$^{\triangle9}$	Cma^7 + M9 (MM7 + M9)
Dmin^9, Dmi^9, Dm^9, d^9, d^{-9}	Dmi^7 + M9 (mm7 + M9)
Dmin^{11}, Dmi^{11}, Dm^{11}, d^{11}, d^{-11}	Dmi^7 + M9 + P11 (mm7 + M9 + P11)
G^9	G^7 + M9 (Mm7 + M9)

Extensions to dominant seventh (Mm7) chords

Extensions appear most frequently with the Mm7 chord. Look at the chart below and play each extension of G^7.

Example: Extensions of G7

Lead-sheet notation	Play this Mm7 chord . . .	plus the interval(s) below.	Optional additional interval(s)
G7(♭9)	complete G7 (G-B-D-F)	m9 (A♭)	
G7(♯9)	complete G7	A9 (A♯)	
G7(♭5)	incomplete G7 (G-B-F)	d5 (D♭)	M9 or m9 (A or A♭)
G7(♯5)	incomplete G7	A5 (D♯)	M9 (A)
G7(♯11)	complete G7	M9 + A11 (A + C♯)	M13 (E)
G13	complete or incomplete G7	M9 + M13 (A + E)	
G7(♭13)	incomplete G7	M9 + m13 (A + E♭)	

The ♭5 and ♯11 are enharmonic equivalents, but are notated differently to indicate the way they tend to resolve. The same concept applies to ♯5 and ♭13. A quick way to get satisfying voicings is to put the root, seventh, and third in the bass clef and the remaining tones in the treble. Play these voicings of extended dominant harmonies.

Now perform each chord below, voicing it several different ways. Some chords have four voices, but many require more.

(a) Bmi7   (d) A7(♯11)   (g) B♭mi9   (j) F♯13   (m) Cmi7

(b) C♯ma9   (e) A♭ma$^9_6$ (h) E♭7(♭13)   (k) Ami9   (n) Gadd6

(c) F7(♭9)   (f) Dma9   (i) Emi11   (l) E7(♯9)   (o) D7(♯5)

Lesson 20: Other Chromatic Harmony (Chapters 29ff.)

A. Chromatic sequences
Return to Lesson 15. Review each diatonic sequence (e.g., A (1)), then learn its corresponding chromatic variation (e.g., A (2)).

B. Modulating with sequences
For each exercise below, choose tonic key signatures ranging from three flats to three sharps.

(1) Follow the procedure from Lesson 17, but in step 2, link the keys with the descending-fifth sequence. Lesson 15 A (2) shows how to alter this sequence in order to modulate.

Example: Modulate from I to V with the descending-fifth sequence

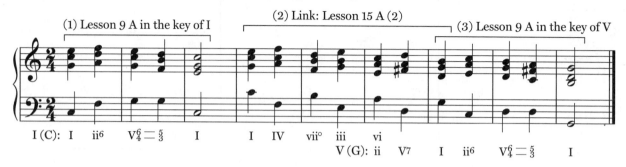

Now modulate from the tonic to the destination keys specified below, linking them with the descending-fifth sequence.

(a) I to V (b) I to vi (c) I to IV (d) I to ii (e) i to III (f) i to v (g) i to iv (h) i to VI

(2) Modulate from I to vi. Study Lesson 15 B (2) to link the keys with the chromatic descending-third sequence.

(3) Modulate from the tonic to the specified keys below. Study Lesson 15 D (2)–(3) to link the keys below with the chromatic ascending 5–6 sequence.

(a) I to V (b) I to vi (c) I to IV (d) I to ii

C. Common-tone embellishing chords

For each example, perform chords 1–3, then play chord 2 only. Beneath the staff are different ways to analyze these chords, but the lowest level, prolonged I, is all that is necessary.

Example 1:

Common-tone diminished seventh chord, CT°7

A CT°7 occurs when a major triad's third and fifth are embellished with chromatic lower neighbors and a sixth is added above the common-tone bass. Chord 2 sounds like a diminished seventh chord, but does not function as one. If it did, it would resolve to a D minor chord.

Example 2:

Common-tone augmented-sixth chord, CT A6

A CT A6 occurs when the doubled fifth of a major triad is embellished with chromatic upper *and* lower neighbors, and its third is embellished with a chromatic lower neighbor. Chord 2 sounds like a Gr6, but does not function as one. If it did, it would resolve to some form of the dominant chord.

Play I–CT°7–I–CT A⁶–I in these major keys: D, G, F, C, E♭, A.

D. Chromatic voice exchange and chromaticized cadential $^6_4$

Model: Perform this example and listen especially to the voice exchange (VE) and cadential $^6_4$.

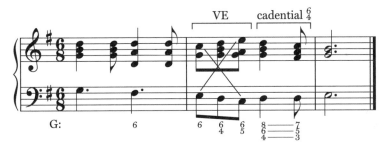

Now perform this variation and listen for their chromatic alteration. The interrupted cadential $^6_4$ may also be notated V$^{6-}_{4-}$ vii°7/vi–vi or V$^{6-}_{4-}$ vi:vii°7 i.

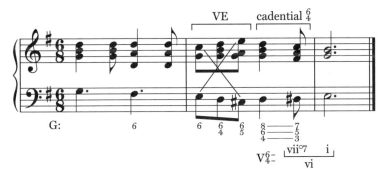

(1) Memorize the model and its variation.

(2) In m. 2 of the model's melody, employ modal mixture by substituting *le* (♭$\hat{6}$) for *la* (6).

(3) Perform the model and its variation in the parallel minor, changing accidentals as appropriate to the key. Note that the chromatic variation will produce a Gr⁶ in m. 2.

(4) Transpose exercises (1)–(3) to keys from three flats to three sharps.

Part IV Keyboard Lessons

When studying this chapter,	review Lesson(s)	then complete Lesson(s)
33	1, 2, 3	
34		21 A
35	21 A	21 B, C, & D
36	all of 21	
37–40	all of 21	

Lesson 21: Unordered Pitch-Class Sets

Perform the examples below, or listen to the recordings on your DVD ("Part IV Keyboard").

Example 1: Alexander Scriabin, *Prelude*, Op. 59, No. 2 (mm. 1–3a)

Example 2: Scriabin, *Prelude*, Op. 59, No. 2 (mm. 12–13a)

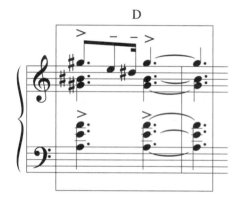

Example 3: Scriabin, *Prelude*, Op. 67, No. 2 (mm. 1–3)

In examples 1 and 3, compare sets A and B. Your ears (and eyes) reveal them to be the same collections, though reversed in order. Since these preludes were composed years apart, clearly Scriabin treats sets A and B as distinct sonorities—unordered pitch-class sets (pcsets).

The pcs of set A are identical in each prelude, as are the pcs of set B. But what if you hear two sets that sound alike but have different pcs? How do you find the relationship between them?

A. Sets related by transposition

Perform example 1 again; consider its highest line to be set C. Perform example 2; consider all its pitches as set D. Play each in its original order, then from lowest to highest. Can you hear that D is a transposition of C by six semitones?

Set C, original order   Play from lowest to highest. Set D, original order Play from lowest to highest.
                       (no duplicated pcs)

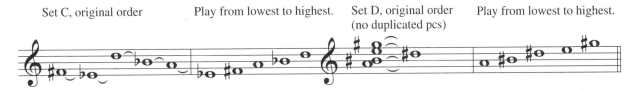

Until you become familiar with sounds like these, it may be hard to hear such relationships. One method that will help is to find each set's **normal order**: its most compact form.

Finding a set's normal order: To find the normal order of set C, first play its pitches in order from lowest to highest, as before. Then play and notate each rotation of set C (move the lowest pitch to the top for each new rotation). The rotation that ascends from D is the normal order, because it has the smallest outside interval (from D to B♭). Write the pc integers beneath each pitch of the normal order. Notate normal order with curly braces: C {2 3 6 9 t}.

Rotations of set C   Normal order

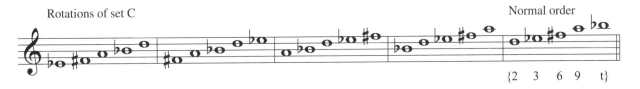

{2 3 6 9 t}

Now play the rotations of set D to find its normal order.

Rotations of set D   Normal order

{8 9 0 3 4}

The rotation with the smallest outside interval ascends from G♯: {8 9 0 3 4}. Play the normal order of sets C and D, and listen to the interval succession for each: +1, +3, +3, +1. Sets whose normal orders have the same succession of intervals are related by *transposition*. To determine their exact transposition:

List the elements of set D (the second set you hear).	{8 9 0 3 4}
Subtract the elements of set C (the first set you hear).	– {2 3 6 9 t}
This reveals the number of semitones of transposition.	6 6 6 6 6

If an element in set D is smaller than the element in C that is being subtracted from it, add 12 to D's element: rather than 0-6, 3-9, and 4-t, subtract 12-6, 15-9, and 16-t (mod 12).

Notating sets equivalent by transposition: Notate this relationship as D = T₆C. T stands for "transposition," and the number after indicates the interval of transposition in semi-tones.

B. Sets related by inversion

Play example 3 again; consider the first five *distinct* pitches of its highest line to be set E. Now compare set E with set A from example 1. First, realize A's pcs within the span of one octave, then play the rotations of A to find its normal order. One possibility appears below.

Best normal order: Three rotations have the same smallest outside interval. When this happens, choose as best normal order the rotation with the smallest intervals (often semitones) closely packed at one end or the other. In this case, the rotation that ascends from F♯ has a semitone between the first two pitches, making it the best normal order: A{6 7 9 0 3}.

Now perform the rotations of set E to find its normal order.

Here too, three rotations show the same smallest outside interval. In this case, the rotation that ascends from F♯ has a semitone between the last two pitches, making it the best normal order: E{6 9 0 2 3}.

Compare the successive pitch intervals of the sets: for set A, the pitch intervals ascend +1, +2, +3, +3; and for E, they ascend +3, +3, +2, +1. When the interval successions of two normal orders are identical but *reversed* in order, the two sets are related by *inversion*. Take these final steps to find their exact relationship:

List the elements of A.	{6 7 9 0 3}
List the elements of E in reverse order	+ {3 2 0 9 6}
(because we already know E is related by inversion).	
Add the elements to reveal the relation.	9 9 9 9 9

Notating sets equivalent by inversion: Notate this relationship as E = T₉IA. The I indicates "inversion" and ₉ is the **index number**—the number obtained when the pcs are added together.

Again, with transpositions you subtract the elements, and with inversions you add them. In performing these operations, if you get a number larger than 11 or smaller than 0, subtract or add 12 to keep the result between 0 and 11.

C. Interval-class vectors

At the keyboard, play new trichord sets F { 7 9 2 } and G { 2 4 9 }. One possible realization is shown below. To identify an interval class (ic), find the shortest possible distance between two pcs as measured in semitones. For example, in set F the pcs G and D might be separated by 19, 7, or 5 semitones. Because 5 is the smallest distance, G and D are members of ic 5. Now determine all the interval classes by playing each pair of pitches. In each trichord, you hear one ic 2 and two ic 5s.

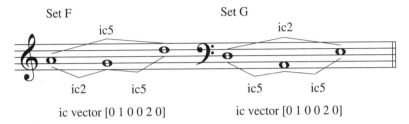

An **ic vector** summarizes the interval-class content of any set. To make one, write interval classes 1–6 in one row and the number of occurrences of each ic underneath.

Interval class:	ic1	ic2	ic3	ic4	ic5	ic6
Number of occurrences:	0	1	0	0	2	0

Once you complete this tally, take the bottom row as the ic vector: [010020]. Because sets F and G share the same ic vector, they share the same interval content, which means they sound alike.

D. Identifying sets as members of set classes

A **set class** (SC) consists of all transpositions and inversions of a particular pcset. Since it would be cumbersome to refer to a SC by listing all its members, one pcset—called its **prime form**—represents the entire group.

1. Identifying transpositions of the prime form

Play example 1, and review how you found the normal order of set C {2 3 6 9 t}. Then play the first pc of the normal order, but call it 0. Play up the chromatic scale from the first pc, counting the number of semitones between each pitch and the first, as shown below. These numbers, 01478, are the pcs of the prime form—Forte SC 5-22. Counting from zero in this way is called "movable zero." You can obtain the same result by subtracting the first element of set C from every element, but movable zero may seem more musically intuitive. Write a set's prime form between square brackets: [0 1 4 7 8].

"Movable zero"

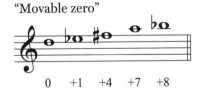

Subtracting the first element

C { 2 3 6 9 t }
− 2 2 2 2 2
_____
   0 1 4 7 8

Now play example 2 and review how you found the normal order of set D { 8 9 0 3 4 }. Apply movable zero or subtract D's first element from each element to determine the prime form. Like C, D also belongs to Forte SC 5-22 [0 1 4 7 8].

2. Identifying inversions of the prime form

Play example 3 and review how you found the normal order for set E { 6 9 0 2 3 }. Recall that E's smallest outside interval occurred between its last two pcs, or to its *right* side. Prime forms, however, all show the smallest intervals to the *left* of the set, so set E must be inverted. Call its last pc zero and play *down* the chromatic scale, counting the number of semitones between each element and the highest, as shown below. Set E's prime form is [0 1 3 6 9], Forte SC 5-31.

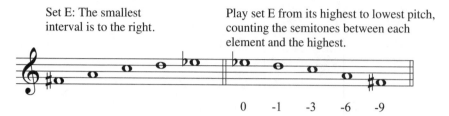

Set E: The smallest interval is to the right.

Play set E from its highest to lowest pitch, counting the semitones between each element and the highest.

        0   -1   -3   -6   -9

Earlier you discovered that set E was equivalent to (an inversion of) set A { 6 7 9 0 3 }, so A must be a member of the same set class. Apply what you have learned to prove this fact. The traditional way of finding the prime form of an inverted set is as follows.

Reverse the elements of E:	{3 2 0 9 6}
Write the mod12 inverse of each element:	{9 t 0 3 6}
Subtract the first element from each pc in the set:	– 9 9 9 9 9
The result is the inverted set's prime form:	[0 1 3 6 9]

For a few set classes, both the normal and inverted form must be subjected to this procedure to determine the prime form.

In the five examples that follow, work through the process at the keyboard (or other instrument) in order to learn to recognize the sets both aurally and kinesthetically. After you have completed the exercises, check your work against the solutions, which begin on p. 457.

Example 1: Anton Webern, "Nachts" ("At Night"), from *Sechs Lieder* (*Six Songs*), Op. 14

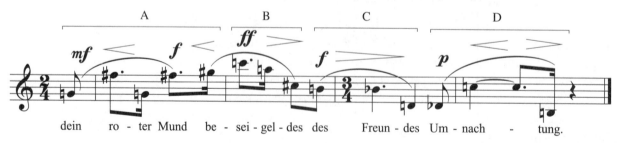

dein   ro - ter Mund   be - sei - gel - des des   Freun - des Um - nach - tung.

Translation: Your red mouth sealed the friend's madness.

Set A   Normal order { ___ ___ ___ } ic vector [___ ___ ___ ___ ___ ___] prime form [___ ___ ___] Forte SC 3-__

Set B   Normal order { ___ ___ ___ } ic vector [___ ___ ___ ___ ___ ___] prime form [___ ___ ___] Forte SC 3-__

Set C   Normal order { ___ ___ ___ } ic vector [___ ___ ___ ___ ___ ___] prime form [___ ___ ___] Forte SC 3-__

Set D   Normal order { ___ ___ ___ } ic vector [___ ___ ___ ___ ___ ___] prime form [___ ___ ___] Forte SC 3-__

(a) How are sets A and D equivalent? (For example, A = T$_x$D or A = T$_x$ID; D = T$_x$A or D = T$_x$IA.)

(b) How are sets B and C equivalent?

On your own paper, show the steps you took to answer each question.

Example 2: Webern, "Wiese im Park" ("Meadows in the Park"), from *Four Songs for Voice and Orchestra*, Op. 13

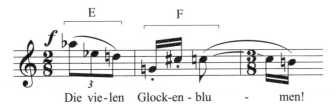

Die vie-len   Glock-en - blu   -   men!

Translation: The many bluebells!

Set E   Normal order { __ __ __ } ic vector [__ __ __ __ __ __] prime form [__ __ __] Forte SC 3-__

Set F   Normal order { __ __ __ } ic vector [__ __ __ __ __ __] prime form [__ __ __] Forte SC 3-__

How are sets E and F equivalent? Show the steps you took to determine their equivalence.

Example 3: Igor Stravinsky, "Action rituelle des ancêtres" ("Ritual Dance of the Elders"), from *The Rite of Spring*

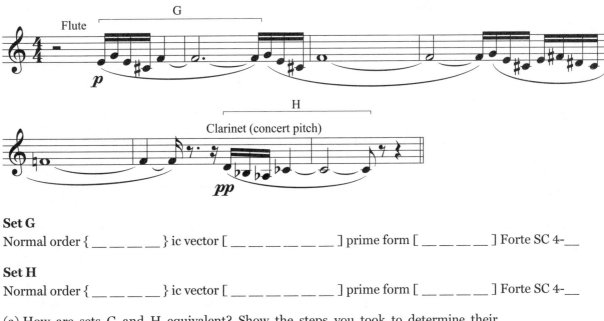

Set G
Normal order { __ __ __ __ } ic vector [__ __ __ __ __ __] prime form [__ __ __ __] Forte SC 4-__

Set H
Normal order { __ __ __ __ } ic vector [__ __ __ __ __ __] prime form [__ __ __ __] Forte SC 4-__

(a) How are sets G and H equivalent? Show the steps you took to determine their equivalence.

(b) Combine the pcs of sets G and H to make a scale. What is the name of this scale?

Example 4: Stravinsky, "Rondes printanières" ("Spring Rounds") and "Action rituelle des ancêtres," from *The Rite of Spring*

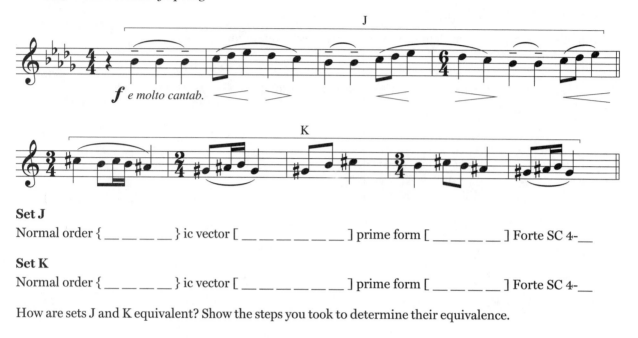

Set J

Normal order { _ _ _ _ } ic vector [_ _ _ _ _ _] prime form [_ _ _ _] Forte SC 4-__

Set K

Normal order { _ _ _ _ } ic vector [_ _ _ _ _ _] prime form [_ _ _ _] Forte SC 4-__

How are sets J and K equivalent? Show the steps you took to determine their equivalence.

Example 5: Webern, *Cantata*, Op. 29

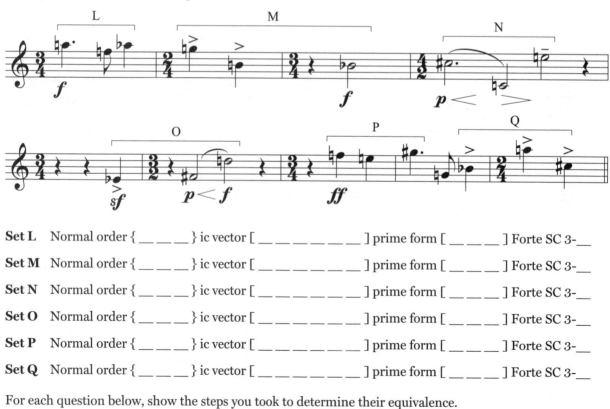

Set L   Normal order { _ _ _ } ic vector [_ _ _ _ _ _] prime form [_ _ _] Forte SC 3-__

Set M   Normal order { _ _ _ } ic vector [_ _ _ _ _ _] prime form [_ _ _] Forte SC 3-__

Set N   Normal order { _ _ _ } ic vector [_ _ _ _ _ _] prime form [_ _ _] Forte SC 3-__

Set O   Normal order { _ _ _ } ic vector [_ _ _ _ _ _] prime form [_ _ _] Forte SC 3-__

Set P   Normal order { _ _ _ } ic vector [_ _ _ _ _ _] prime form [_ _ _] Forte SC 3-__

Set Q   Normal order { _ _ _ } ic vector [_ _ _ _ _ _] prime form [_ _ _] Forte SC 3-__

For each question below, show the steps you took to determine their equivalence.

(a) How are sets M and L equivalent?

(b) How are sets N and L equivalent?

(c) How are sets O and L equivalent?

(d) How are sets P and L equivalent?

(e) How are sets Q and L equivalent?

Solutions

Example 1: Anton Webern, "Nachts" ("At Night"), from *Sechs Lieder* (*Six Songs*), Op. 14

Set A   Normal order { 6 7 8 }   ic vector [210000]   prime form [0 1 2]   Forte SC 3-1

Set B   Normal order { 9 0 1 }   ic vector [101100]   prime form [0 1 4]   Forte SC 3-4

Set C   Normal order { t e 2 }   ic vector [101100]   prime form [0 1 4]   Forte SC 3-4

Set D   Normal order { e 0 1 }   ic vector [210000]   prime form [0 1 2]   Forte SC 3-1

(a) How are sets A and D equivalent?   (b) How are sets B and C equivalent?

$$\begin{array}{ccc} \text{D}\{e\,0\,1\} & \text{or} & \text{A}\{6\,7\,8\} \\ -\text{A}\{6\,7\,8\} & & -\text{D}\{e\,0\,1\} \\ \hline \text{T}\;\overline{5\,5\,5} & & \text{T}\;\overline{7\,7\,7} \end{array}$$

$$\begin{array}{c} \text{C}\{t\,e\,2\} \\ +\text{B}\{1\,0\,9\}\,(\text{elements reversed}) \\ \hline \text{index}\;\overline{e\,e\,e} \end{array}$$

$$D = T_5A \qquad\qquad A = T_7D$$

$$B = T_eIC \text{ or } C = T_eIB$$

Example 2: Webern, "Wiese im Park" ("Meadows in the Park"), from *Four Songs for Voice and Orchestra*, Op. 13

Set E   Normal order { 2 3 8 }   ic vector [100011]   prime form [0 1 6]   Forte SC 3-5

Set F   Normal order { 7 0 1 }   ic vector [100011]   prime form [0 1 6]   Forte SC 3-5

How are sets E and F equivalent?

$$\begin{array}{c} \text{E}\{2\,3\,8\} \\ +\text{F}\{1\,0\,7\}\,(\text{elements reversed}) \\ \hline \text{index}\;\overline{3\,3\,3} \end{array} \qquad\qquad E = T_3IF \text{ or } F = T_3IE$$

Example 3: Igor Stravinsky, "Action rituelle des ancêtres" ("Ritual Dance of the Elders"), from *The Rite of Spring*

Set G   Normal order { 1 4 5 7 }   ic vector [112101]   prime form [0 2 3 6]   Forte SC 4-12

Set H   Normal order { 8 t e 2 }   ic vector [112101]   prime form [0 2 3 6]   Forte SC 4-12

(a) How are sets G and H equivalent?   (b) Combine the pcs of sets G and H to make a scale. What is the name of this scale? octatonic

$$\begin{array}{c} \text{G}\{1\,4\,5\,7\} \\ +\text{H}\{2\,e\,t\,8\}\,(\text{elements reversed}) \\ \hline \text{index}\;\overline{3\,3\,3\,3} \end{array}$$

$$G = T_3IH \text{ or } H = T_3IG$$

Example 4: Stravinsky, "Rondes printanières" ("Spring Rounds") and "Action rituelle des ancêtres," from *The Rite of Spring*

Set J Normal order { t 0 1 3 }   ic vector [122010]   prime form [0 2 3 5] Forte SC 4-10

Set K Normal order { 8 t e 1 }   ic vector [122010]   prime form [0 2 3 5] Forte SC 4-10

How are sets J and K equivalent?

J { t 0 1 3 }   or   J { t 0 1 3 }   K { 8 t e 1 }
+ K { 1 e t 8 } (elements reversed)   − K { 8 t e 1 }   − J { t 0 1 3 }
index $\overline{e\,e\,e\,e}$ J = T_eIK or K = T_eIJ   T $\overline{2\,2\,2\,2}$ T $\overline{t\,t\,t\,t}$ J = T_2K or K = T_tJ

Example 5: Webern, *Cantata*, Op. 29

Set L Normal order { 5 8 9 }   ic vector [101100]   prime form [0 1 4]   Forte SC 3-3

Set M Normal order { 7 t e }   ic vector [101100]   prime form [0 1 4]   Forte SC 3-3

Set N Normal order { 0 1 4 }   ic vector [101100]   prime form [0 1 4]   Forte SC 3-3

Set O Normal order { 2 3 6 }   ic vector [101100]   prime form [0 1 4]   Forte SC 3-3

Set P Normal order { 4 5 8 }   ic vector [101100]   prime form [0 1 4]   Forte SC 3-3

Set Q Normal order { 9 t 1 }   ic vector [101100]   prime form [0 1 4]   Forte SC 3-3

(a) How are sets M and L equivalent?

M { 7 t e }
− L { 5 8 9 }
T $\overline{2\,2\,2}$ M = T_2L or L = T_2M

(b) How are sets N and L equivalent?

N { 0 1 4 }
+ L { 9 8 5 } (elements reversed)
index $\overline{9\,9\,9}$ N = T_9IL or L = T_9IN

(c) How are sets O and L equivalent?

O { 2 3 6 }
− L { 9 8 5 } (elements reversed)
index $\overline{e\,e\,e}$ O = T_eIL or L = T_eIO

(d) How are sets P and L equivalent?

P { 4 5 8 }
+ L { 9 8 5 } (elements reversed)
index $\overline{1\,1\,1}$ P = T_1IL or L = T_1IP

(e) How are sets Q and L equivalent?

Q { 9 t 1 }
+ L { 9 8 5 } (elements reversed)
index $\overline{6\,6\,6}$ Q = T_6IL or L = T_6IQ

Credits

Index of Music Examples